✳

THE
INCREDIBLE
BIRTHS
OF JESUS

THE
INCREDIBLE
BIRTHS
OF JESUS

*

EDWARD REAUGH SMITH

℮ Anthroposophic Press

Published by Anthroposophic Press
3390 Route 9, Hudson, N.Y. 12534

Library of Congress Cataloging-in-Publication Data

Smith, Edward Reaugh, 1932–
    The incredible births of Jesus / Edward Reaugh Smith.
        p.   cm.
    Includes bibliographical references.
    ISBN 0-88010-448-1 (pbk.)
    1. Jesus Christ—Anthroposophical interpretations.
    2. Jesus Christ—Nativity—Miscellanea. 3. Anthroposophy.
    I. Title.
    BP596.J4S55   1998
    299'.935--dc21   98-37290
                                                            CIP

Printed in the United States of America

CONTENTS

Introduction by Will Marsh   7

Foreword   25

The Incredible Births of Jesus   29

   The Valley of the Shadow   29

   Christmas Day   31

   Seeming Conflicts and Differences   32

   Two Different Lines of Descent   37

   Seeing, Hearing and Understanding   38

   Two Critical Concepts   42

   Two Common Features   47

   The Solomon Jesus Child of Matthew's Gospel 48

   The Nathan Jesus Child of Luke's Gospel   52

   How the Solomon Jesus and Nathan Jesus Became One 65

   From Jesus of Nazareth to Jesus Christ   72

   The Mystery of the Marys   73

   Conclusion   76

(Continued on next page)

Epilogue   *78*

    Why Now?   *78*

    The Archangel Michael   *83*

Biblical Accounts of the Birth of Jesus   *93*

    The Gospel According to Matthew   *93*

    The Gospel According to Luke   *97*

INTRODUCTION

by Will Marsh

To read the biblical accounts of the birth of Jesus in the Gospels of Matthew and Luke is to enter the realm of mystery. A human being was born, into whom a spiritual being of the highest order, the Son of God, would later descend and indwell for three and a half years. How are we to go about understanding this event, so beyond our normal understanding? What human vehicle could be adequate to undertake the indwelling of the Son of God? What sort of human being was the babe born in Bethlehem?

The place to begin is with the Gospels themselves. We are told that the Jesus child was conceived by a virgin when the Holy Spirit came upon her and the power of the Most High overshadowed her. In Matthew the nature of the conception is made known only after the fact; Mary is "found to be with child of the Holy Spirit," and when Joseph, her betrothed, is troubled by this, an Angel appears in a dream to tell him the nature of the conception. In Luke, the Archangel Gabriel appears directly to Mary beforehand to tell her what will happen, and this event has been foreshadowed by Gabriel's appearance to Zechariah telling him that his wife Elizabeth, a kinswoman of Mary, will bear him a son, who is to be named John. Elizabeth was previously barren and is well past childbearing age, so we are presented with two pregnancies normally outside the range of human possibility. And when the pregnant Mary, arriving for a visit, greets the pregnant Elizabeth, the babe in Elizabeth's womb leaps in recognition, so Jesus and John the Baptist are connected even before they are born. We are told that Mary stayed with Elizabeth for about three months, which means she would have been there until just before John's birth. In both accounts, Angels and an Archangel appear to humans, acting as messengers from God, and in Luke an Angel is joined by a multitude of the Heavenly Host to announce Jesus' birth to the shepherds, so we see that many levels of the Spiritual Hierarchies are involved in the birth. Cosmic events are also involved, for a special star appears in the heavens. In Matthew the child is first visited by three kingly wise men from the East who have special knowledge that has enabled them to recognize and follow the star, and who bring special gifts, while in Luke the child is born in a humble stable and the first visitors we are told of are humble shepherds.

There are many things about the Gospel accounts that cause us to pause. It seems easier for us to understand that the Son of God could somehow appear to us in human form than it is for us to understand that a being could be both fully human in every sense and the Son of God. Given the unique spiritual mission that awaited him, we want to know more about the baby Jesus himself, how he acted, how he grew, what sort of child he became and what his childhood was like, how he interacted with the children and adults in his village and with the natural world, how he was trained, and what he was like as an adolescent and a young man—but here the Gospels present us with almost a total blank. Luke is the only Evangelist who tells us anything about the childhood, and he relates only one event, the teaching by the twelve-year-old Jesus in the Temple; the next event in Luke's narrative is the Baptism, when Jesus is about thirty years old. Matthew mentions only the flight of the holy family into Egypt immediately after Jesus' birth to avoid Herod's slaughter of the innocents, and their eventual return to live in Nazareth, then skips to the Baptism. Mark and John (after the Prologue) both begin with the descent of the Spirit at the Baptism. We are left with much to ponder.

Although we tend to conflate the Nativity narratives in Matthew and in Luke into one picture, we note immediately upon comparing them that many of the events, which all seem so important, appear only in Matthew or only in Luke. Mary is barely mentioned in Matthew, which, after the opening genealogy, focuses on the Angel's appearance to Joseph, the visit of the wise men, and the reactions of Herod. In Luke's account, Mary is the most prominent figure, recognized as "favored one" and "blessed among women" by Archangel and human alike; she is also shown to have had a deep awareness of what was going on, for she knew that her soul "magnifies the Lord," and she "kept all these things, and pondered them in her heart." How can the two Nativity accounts be so dissimilar? Even the genealogy of Jesus, which would seem to be straightforward, is not the same in the two accounts and is completely different for the generations between David and Joseph. Surely both Evangelists would be aware of most of the key elements of this central event in their message, equalled in importance only by the events surrounding the Mystery of Golgotha? The descriptions of the Crucifixion and the Resurrection are nearly identical in the synoptic Gospels and are very similar in John; the same is true for the Baptism. Many other events of the ministry of Jesus Christ are described in similar terms in the synoptic Gospels. Why is that not the case for the Nativity?

The differences between the Matthew and Luke accounts are so great that they almost seem to be describing the births of two different children. And, as hard to comprehend as it may be, that is precisely what Edward Smith tells us is the case—there were two Jesus babies, the one in Matthew born of the kingly lineage of David's son Solomon, and the one in Luke born of the priestly lineage of David's son Nathan. How this can be, how it came about, what became of the two children so that there was only one, why this has been generally unknown until this century, what it means for a true understanding of the nature of Jesus Christ, of Christianity, and of human and world evolution—all are discussed in *The Incredible Births of Jesus*. It is an amazing story.

Edward Smith, now "retired" after a successful career as a lawyer and businessman, has been a lifelong student of the Scriptures and of theology, and has long pondered them in his mind and in his heart. While still a young man, he was given a near-death experience on a hospital operating table, during which he was enveloped in what he describes as a tangible light and love that he felt as the immediate presence of the Christ. This experience strengthened his faith and gave him spiritual assurance as he continued to struggle with the issues raised by his continuing study of the Bible, which he taught as the leader of an adult Sunday School class for over twenty-five years. Growing increasingly unsatisfied with mainstream theological interpretations, he was led in the mid-1980s to reconsider reincarnation as a possible key to understanding the many dilemmas the Bible presents to the serious seeker, and began to study the subject with his usual intensity. In the course of this study, he came across the anthroposophy of Rudolf Steiner, and finding in it many of the answers he sought, he devoted six years to investigating Steiner's "spiritual science." He now sees it as his main task to present the anthroposophical understanding of the Bible to mainstream Christianity; *The Incredible Births of Jesus* and his longer, recently published *The Burning Bush* are the first steps in that direction.

Reading Edward Smith's presentation of such a radical new way of looking at the Nativity, we naturally want to know more about its source, the spiritual research done by Rudolf Steiner in the first two decades of this century. Rudolf Steiner (1861–1925) was an Austrian philosopher, cognitive scientist, and spiritual teacher, probably best known in this country, to the extent that he is known at all, as the founder of the Waldorf School movement and the biodynamic agriculture movement. From childhood he had experienced not only the world of sense perceptions that we all experience, but also another dimension not based on sense perceptions, which he came to know as the spiritual world. He could not ignore this experience of the other dimension, as most children are taught to do in our rationalistic, materialistic culture, and as an adolescent he set himself the task of understanding how these two worlds, the sense world and the spiritual world, are connected; further, he felt he had to gain this understanding by using the exacting scientific approach of the natural sciences. To achieve this he undertook a rigorous scientific training, focused on the natural sciences, mathematics, and an experimental, phenomenological study of science and epistemology—how we know what we know. While in his twenties, Steiner was asked to edit the scientific writings of Johann Wolfgang von Goethe for a new German edition of the Complete Works. (Goethe, great poet and dramatist that he was, felt that his scientific writings, such as *The Metamorphosis of Plants,* were his most important work.) Goethe had developed a phenomenological, participatory approach to science, in which the observer's qualitative experience of nature is not treated as just subjective but is taken as a primary perception as much as the quantitative; in this method the part can only be understood in its relation to the whole.[1] Steiner, who knew from his own experience that it was within the capacity of the human being to know the world's actual spiritual reality, found in Goethe's science a key to developing a scientific methodology by which one could move from the sense world of ordinary consciousness to the recognition of the world of pure thinking that lies behind it, and thence to the higher world of spirit: he had bridged the gulf between the sense world and the spiritual world. He laid out this methodology in *Intuitive Thinking as a Spiritual Path: A Philosophy of Freedom* (1894), which is both an original contribution to cognitive science and the basis for all his spiritual researches.

Then, as Rudolf Steiner wrote in his *Autobiography*, he was granted an experience that initiated him into the reality of Christ in cosmic evolution: "Conscious knowledge of true Christianity began to dawn in me. Around the turn of the century this knowledge grew deeper.... This experience culminated in my standing in the spiritual presence of the Mystery of Golgotha in a most profound and solemn festival of knowledge."[2] The experience convinced him that the time had come to begin elaborating and making available the results of his spiritual researches. He found an understanding audience in the Theosophical Society, which had been founded

---

1. See Henri Bortoft, *The Wholeness of Nature*, Lindisfarne Press, Hudson, NY, 1996.
2. *Rudolf Steiner: An Autobiography*, Steinerbooks, Blauvelt, NY, 1980, chap. 16.

by H. P. Blavatsky to work for the renewal of spiritual knowledge, and linked himself with it, under the condition that he
would have complete autonomy and independence, as the Sec-
retary of the German Section until 1912, when he founded
the Anthroposophical Society. Before the First World War,
Steiner's researches, lectures, and writings were mostly concerned with the evolution and true nature of the human
being, the development of the human capacity for knowing
the spiritual world, and the development of an understanding
of true Christianity. After the devastation of the war, he felt
that social renewal was the most pressing spiritual need and
shifted his focus there, touching in one way or another on
most areas of human endeavor.

Between 1906 and 1912 Rudolf Steiner gave several long
lecture series on Christianity and the Gospels, and these, particularly *The Gospel of St. Matthew* and *The Gospel of St. Luke*,
are the primary sources of the material that Edward Smith
presents below. The lectures were based on Steiner's spiritual
researches using his consciously trained and directed clairvoyance, which somehow made what he investigated a living
experience for him—he stressed over and over that he spoke
and wrote of nothing he had not experienced himself. Experience, he said, is the sole guide to reality and truth. It should
be pointed out that this conscious clairvoyance has nothing
to do with either mediumship or unconscious channeling,
which could often be found in the Theosophical Society at
that time and in the New Age movement today. Steiner
insisted that conscious clairvoyance, as well as related faculties of inspiration and intuition that give direct access to the
spiritual world, while unusual in our time, are not special
gifts, but are innate possibilities within every human being,
undeveloped organs of perception that can be developed by

training the thinking, feeling, and willing. Steiner's basic writings, the "basic books" of anthroposophy, or spiritual science, lay out how such training can be undertaken, starting from where we are with short exercises that are surprisingly simple on the surface, yet require disciplined practice.[3] One final point should be made: Given the sheer volume of Rudolf Steiner's writings and lectures, and their radical nature for our ordinary consciousness, it is important not to take their content as information—we should not and are not expected to accept them passively or on blind faith. Rather they should be seen as records of the experiences of someone farther along the path, which can light and prod us along our own paths so that we too can participate more fully, freely, and consciously in the divine and human world process.

The things Edward Smith tells us can be seen as part of a revolutionary movement in Christianity in this century brought about by startling discoveries of long-lost early Christian documents, documents that support the understanding of Christianity presented below. The libraries found earlier in this century at Nag Hammadi and at Qumran have shown beyond reasonable doubt that at the time of Christian beginnings these worlds were intermingled. By restoring the living context of early Christianity, these discoveries are providing keys necessary for a fuller understanding of the role and meaning of Christianity in human evolution and of the teachings of Jesus Christ as given in the Gospels and the writings of

---

3. The developmental path is most clearly laid out in *How to Know Higher Worlds*. The other basic books are *Intuitive Thinking as a Spiritual Path, Theosophy, An Outline of Esoteric Science,* and *Christianity as Mystical Fact.* These, and the Gospel lectures, are available from Anthroposophic Press, Hudson, NY.

Paul. They are also giving a clearer picture of the world Jesus was born into, and it is a different picture than the one we have been given by traditional Christian doctrine.

In 1947 a Bedouin shepherd stumbled upon a cave in a cliff at Qumran, near the northwestern shore of the Dead Sea. In the cave he found several large jars containing long scrolls, some twenty feet or longer. His discovery set off a search by scholars and peasants that unearthed numerous other scrolls in the vicinity. These Dead Sea Scrolls, as they became known, proved to be preserved ancient manuscripts, in Hebrew, of biblical and other texts, which were eventually determined by scholars to have been the library of a community of Jewish Essenes, dating from the first or second century B.C. Complete scrolls or fragments of all of the books of the Old Testament, except the Book of Esther, were found, as well as much of the Old Testament apocrypha and pseudepigrapha, including the *Book of Jubilees,* the *Book of Enoch,* and the *Testaments of the Twelve Patriarchs.* In addition to these familiar books, there were also texts of teachings and practices of the Essenes, who had been little known before, although Philo of Alexandria, Josephus, and a few other contemporaries had written briefly of them. Philo (*Every Good Man Is Free,* XII) wrote that they were Jews living in Judea and Syria who derived their name "from their piety." They were pacifists who lived communally without private property or covetousness, did not sacrifice living animals, and were above all devoted to the study of God and to preserving their minds in a state of holiness and purity. Despite the previous lack of knowledge about the Essenes, they must have played an important role in Jewish society, for Josephus (*The Jewish War,* II) placed them on an equal footing with the Sadducees and the Pharisees, the major religious parties of the time, and there was an Essene quarter in Jerusalem and an Essene gate.

The *Community Rule* found at Qumran contains the central teachings of the Essenes. Part of it lays out strict rules for living together in a spiritually vital society, some of them similar to those in the discourses of Jesus Christ in chapters 10 and 18 of the Gospel of Matthew. These ordinances were based on a strict, spiritualized interpretation of the Torah that disagreed with the interpretation of the Sadducees and the Pharisees. Here we come to the key element of Essene teaching, for their understanding of the Scriptures was based on an "illumination" attained through initiation; only those who had undergone initiation could remain in the community beyond an initial probationary period. The preparatory stages for this initiation, described in the *Community Rule,* involved a lengthy period of probation, study, and purification, followed by initiatory rites that included repeated baptism by full submersion and instruction in secret knowledge, leading to direct experience of the spiritual world. We see in this initiatory process the same elements—strict spiritual disciplines, initiatory rites, the experience of illumination—found in the ancient pagan Mysteries that flourished in Mesopotamia, Egypt, Syria, Asia Minor, and later in Greece. That is to say, the Essenes were a Jewish sect carrying on the ancient Mystery tradition in the heartland of Judea just before the birth of Jesus—but the Essenes added an adherence to the Law and an emphasis on community that came from their Jewish heritage.

Essene initiation brought about a *metanoia,* a profound change of consciousness experienced as an inner rebirth that bestowed a divine knowledge. Initiates were known as "sons of Light" and joined in a cosmic struggle with the powers of Darkness. The Essenes' esoteric understanding of the Old

Testament was based on their ability to see the cosmic struggle between the forces of Light and Darkness that lies behind the events narrated there. Their library also included the pseude-pigraphical *Book of Enoch,* which describes this cosmic strug-gle as well as a vision of the heavenly spheres and higher realms. The Essenes used a Sun-based calendar, like the one described in *Enoch,* not the traditional Moon-based Jewish calendar, so the proper days for the observance of the holy feasts were another point of disagreement with the Sadducees and the Pharisees. In their struggle with the forces of Dark-ness, the sons of Light were aided by a knowledge of esoteric sciences, particularly astrology and occult physiology; frag-mentary technical texts on these subjects were found at Qum-ran.[4] As we will see, this esoteric knowledge was used in preparing for the coming of the Christ Being to Earth.

There seems to have been a higher stage of initiation among the Essenes that gave one the right to attend a ritual sacred meal, anticipating the bread and wine that would be shared with the Messiah. But here the story takes another twist, for the Essenes expected two Messiahs. There is a pas-sage in the *Community Rule* specifying that the "men of holi-ness" shall be ruled by the Law and the precepts of the community "until there shall come the Prophet and the Mes-siahs of Aaron and Israel." The Messiah of Israel (or Jacob) is the kingly Davidic Messiah expected by traditional Judaism, but the Messiah of Aaron would be of the priestly lineage and had a more universal meaning for the Essenes, in that he

---

4. My description of the Essene teaching is based on Andrew Welburn's *The Beginnings of Christianity,* Floris Books, Edinburgh, 1995, chaps. 2 and 3. Translations of the Dead Sea Scrolls can be found in Geza Vermes, *The Dead Sea Scrolls in English,* Penguin Books, Harmondsworth, 1987.

would express their special wisdom and fulfill their esoteric vision. Two Messiahs are also mentioned in the *Testaments of the Patriarchs*. Some scrolls from Qumran show this expectation in a different light, for the *Damascus Document* and an interpretation of the Psalms seem to foretell a compound figure in whom the kingly and priestly Messiahs would be joined in one person. The Essene expectation of the coming of the Messiah and of his nature shows influences not only from the Jewish Old Testament tradition but also from the Zoroastrian tradition of ancient Persia, where there were prophecies or legends of the coming of as many as twelve "Saviors." But the forces of Darkness would only be ultimately overcome with the coming of a "world Savior" who would embody the "two dignities, Kingship and the Good Religion."[5]

There is also an obvious connection between the Essene teaching of the struggle between Light and Darkness and the central teaching of the Zoroastrian mythology, the struggle between the two cosmic principles, Ohrmazd, Light, and Ahriman, Darkness. But Andrew Welburn points out that there has been a key change in the Essene teaching, reflecting what has been developing in Judaism throughout Old Testament history. The *Community Rule* (III–IV) says that "the God of Knowledge," from whom "comes all that is and happens," "has created man to govern the world, and has appointed for him two Spirits in which to walk until the time of his visitation: the Spirit of Truth and the Spirit of Falsehood. Those born of Truth spring from a fountain of Light, but those born of falsehood spring from a source of Darkness." Here the two Zoroastrian cosmic principles have been

---

5. Andrew Welburn, *Gnosis: The Mysteries and Christianity,* Floris Books, Edinburgh, 1994, chap. 3.

transformed into "two Spirits in man": the great spiritual struggle has been shifted from the cosmos into the individual human soul. The crucial element in the struggle is now the human being in its ethical individuality. The Essene teaching merged the initiatic knowledge and experience of the divine from the Mystery tradition with the sense of the self, of individual moral responsibility, and of history as the revelation of the mysteries of God that had developed in the Jewish tradition; however the source of morality still lay outside the human being, in the Law. This synthesis represents the first stages of a new religious consciousness.[6]

Still more about the early Christian world has become known in the last twenty years through the analysis of another treasure trove of long-lost writings from that era, which was discovered near Nag Hammadi in upper Egypt before the Qumran find but took longer to become available for study. In December 1945, two brothers digging nitrogenous soil to fertilize their fields near the ancient city of Chenoboskion on the east bank of the Nile unearthed a large sealed earthenware pot. Inside were twelve codices, books of bound papyrus sheets, totaling about fifteen hundred pages. These were impounded for decades in the Cairo Museum and, except for a few tractates that were smuggled to Europe and published by the Jung Institute in Zurich, only became available in English in 1977. The Nag Hammadi Library, as the codices became known, were determined to have most likely been the library of a Valentinian Gnostic sect active in upper Egypt in the early centuries of the Christian era. (*Gnostic* comes from *gnosis,* meaning knowledge, direct spiritual knowledge, but Gnosticism refers to a particular historical movement active

---

6. Welburn, *Beginnings of Christianity,* pp. 49–51.

from the first century B.C. to the third century A.D., believed to have developed out of the oriental mystical tradition of the ancient Mysteries.) Before the Nag Hammadi discovery, the Gnostics were known mainly through the writings of Church Fathers, such as Hippolytus, who quoted Gnostic writings only to show how heretical they were. Now for the first time the Gnostics were allowed to speak for themselves.

The codices were discovered to contain fifty-two tractates, including six that were already known and six duplicates. Ten of the others were fragmentary, but the remaining thirty previously unknown texts were in reasonably good shape. Many of the tractates are Gnostic teachings, but others come from different sources; there is an excerpt from Plato's *Republic* and texts from the Egyptian Hermetic tradition, for example *The Discourse on the Eighth and Ninth* (spheres, or levels of consciousness), a description of the initiatory process that raised the neophyte's consciousness through levels corresponding to the planetary spheres, and higher. Many of the texts are Christian, but written from a decidedly Gnostic point of view, depicting Christ as a cosmic divinity and expressing his teachings and acts in terms of the initiatic Mysteries. These "Gnostic Gospels" have proven controversial, particularly *The Gospel of Thomas,* which claims to be "secret sayings" of Jesus Christ given to the apostle Thomas and written down by Matthias, and *The Gospel of Philip,* which presents a Mystery form of Christianity with an elaborate system of sacraments. It was at first assumed that *The Gospel of Thomas* was derived from the canonical Gospels because many of the sayings were similar, but recent scholarship based on careful textual analysis indicates that it may have been written before them and may even have influenced them. Whether or not this is the case, the Nag Hammadi finds did show that in the second century there was an alternative vision of Christianity that included Mystery teachings and also had more tolerant attitudes in such things as ritual, authority, individual experience, and the role of women.[7]

This is not to say that because Gnosticism contained elements of esoteric Christianity it was esoteric Christianity. Gnosticism was heretical because it did not comprehend or accept the full Christian message. In Gnostic teaching the human being is an alien here on Earth, which is something to be left behind since it was created by a lesser god, a Demiurge. Darkness exists as an eternal second principle, and human beings can escape its influence only by merging their identity with the Light. But without esoteric knowledge, revealed through initiation, human beings would not know the way to salvation; and to become knowers and to participate as knowers in the divine process, they must put aside the delusion of the physical body, of individuality, and of historical reality. In Gnosticism, unlike in Essenism, there was no individual or historical moral struggle. Gnosticism continued to cling to the ancient form of the Mystery tradition, which had fulfilled its mission in human evolution with the coming of Jesus Christ, who established a new Mystery, one that was to be experienced in the open, on the stage of world history. The Gnostics could not accept the historical reality of Jesus Christ or of the Mystery of Golgotha.

One of the most intriguing texts found at Nag Hammadi is *The Apocalypse of Adam,* which is believed to predate the others and not to be a Gnostic text at all. It may be of Essene origin

---

7. Welburn, *Beginnings of Christianity,* chap. 4. Translations of the Nag Hammadi texts are in James M. Robinson, ed., *The Nag Hammadi Library in English,* E. J. Brill, Leiden, 1988.

and is written in the same style as the *Testaments of the Twelve Patriarchs*. In it a seer projects himself back into the past, to the time of Adam, in order to follow the patterns of the cycles of time. It tells, in the form of parables, of thirteen different incarnations of a messenger called "the Illuminator." Andrew Welburn has shown that each parable uses the symbolism of one of the ancient Mysteries and that together they reveal a sequence of incarnations in the different civilizations of the ancient world—Persia, Media, Egypt, India, Assyria, Babylon, Greece, Armenia, Ethiopia. The final incarnation, which still lies in the future for the writer, will combine the special qualities of the different Mystery streams in the person of the Royal Messiah. Welburn goes on to argue convincingly that "the Illuminator" is none other than Zarathustra, founder of the Zoroastrian religion.[8] The significance of this will become apparent in Edward Smith's narrative of the events leading to the Nativity of Jesus.

The Nag Hammadi and Qumran discoveries show that the Mystery tradition was present in a vital form at the birth of Christianity, even in the heartland of Judea. The Essene synthesis of Judaism and the Mystery tradition looked forward and can be said to have prepared for and presaged Christianity, while Gnosticism looked backward and tried to maintain the ancient form of the Mysteries by grafting Christianity onto it. However, both the Essene and the Gnostic paths of salvation were only for the elite, the initiated, and were based on transporting the initiate away from the Earth, to the spiritual realms, to encounter God. That all changed with the appearance of Jesus Christ on Earth. The Christ Being freely

---

8. Welburn, *The Book with Fourteen Seals*, Rudolf Steiner Press, Sussex, 1991; also *Gnosis*, chap. 6.

joined his destiny with earthly and human destiny as "the free helper of humanity, not as a God working from above, but as the firstborn among many."[9] In so doing, he returned to humankind the chance, not possible since the Fall, to become fully human spiritual beings and thereby to heal the rift between the Earth and the spiritual world. But to do so human beings, for their own part, must choose freely and individually to open their hearts to Christ, to join their destinies with him, and to be about the human task of bringing freedom and love into the world.

The Qumran and Nag Hammadi documents provide evidence that the Mystery tradition, and most notably the Essenes, expected and helped prepare for the births of the two Jesus children and the subsequent descent of the Christ Being into Jesus of Nazareth. The Mystery knowledge was suppressed and lost until this century, but without the keys it provides a true understanding of Christianity has not been possible; the result has been confusion and strife, leading finally to the fragmentation, fundamentalism, relativism, and skepticism of our time. Humanity needs to come to a true understanding of Christianity and of Christ Jesus if it is to evolve and assume its proper place in the cosmos. In this radical little book, Edward Smith shows us the first steps toward that understanding, a new Mystery for our time, now not just for the elite few but for all who desire to open their eyes and see.

---

9. Rudolf Steiner, *The Spiritual Hierarchies and the Physical World,* Anthroposophic Press, Hudson, NY, 1996, p. 163.

FOREWORD

At sixty-five years of age I look back upon a life filled with many disciplines, including successful professional careers in law and business and amateur ones in music and athletics. I am blessed with a loving family, a wife of over forty-three years, children and grandchildren, all of whom I am deeply proud of. Since childhood I've been a regular and active church person, though I put no stock in denominationalism. Along with these things, and having felt from youth that the Bible reflected sacred truths, mine has also been a lifetime of studying and teaching the Bible, in a restless search for its deeper meanings—for the truth, regardless of how popular it might be or how much opposition it might encounter, recognizing that truth is seldom accepted by the majority when first revealed. In that pursuit, in the fall of 1988 I happened across a reference to the Austrian, Rudolf Steiner (1861-1925). This book is a result of that discovery.

Recently my book, *The Burning Bush*, was published by the Anthroposophic Press. It is thoroughly documented throughout by extensive references, Biblical and otherwise, as well as numerous study helps. But some have suggested the need for a more simplified version of some of its topics—one that contains essentially no citations or footnotes and flows more easily for the average reader. This book is the result, and addresses the first topic from *The Burning Bush*, namely, "The Nativity." Those who desire to pursue it and its related topics more deeply may refer to the larger work.

What is presented in this book may appear at first quite bizarre. It might help not to be derailed by that circumstance, however, to consider how bizarre the Bible story itself would appear to one who comes upon it for the first time free of tradition and a society that dares not question it. Moreover, one should consider the number of passages that even to such a society are either entirely mysterious and problematical or totally ignored. Mind you, I accept the Bible as a divinely inspired book. I merely question that it can be understood in the vulgar mode of our common vernacular—at least not in a way appropriate for our stage of human development. It will be helpful to accept some concepts tentatively until the whole story unfolds, recognizing that understanding the whole of the birth story also involves some concepts that can only be touched upon lightly in this shorter work. As the picture unfolds, one can be thrilled to experience the feeling that the Bible then becomes one beautiful, integrated spiritual account consistent from beginning to end, its problem passages no longer being so mysterious.

Finally, several have made the suggestion that the word "anthroposophy," not yet found in most dictionaries, be defined. The larger work is called "An Anthroposophical Commentary on the Bible." "Anthroposophy" is the term Rudolf Steiner coined for his intuitive understandings of the spiritual world and its relation to the world we perceive with our ordinary senses. He also called it by the synonymous phrase, "spiritual science." Anthroposophy is a combination of the two Greek root words, *anthropo*, and *sophia*. The latter, with a capital, is defined in our dictionaries as "wisdom," and given a feminine attribute. The Sophia is personified as the feminine "Wisdom" in the first nine chapters of Proverbs. Our common suffix "sophy" derives from it and means "knowledge or thought," as in "philosophy," "theosophy," and the like.

Anthropo should be distinguished from *homo*, a Latin word referring to a two-legged primate. We should think of *homo* as referring to the body, and *anthropo* as referring to that which sets the human being above the animal. It represents the higher aspect, the soul or the soul and the spirit, of the human being. Thus, "anthroposophy" is the wisdom of the soul of the human being.

As you read on, you are embarking upon a new spiritual experience.

The Incredible Births of Jesus

NEW AND DEEPER UNDERSTANDINGS

The Valley of the Shadow

N O STORY IS SO WELL KNOWN, nor perhaps any so little understood, as the birth of Jesus. Its mystery
steals into every heart as days shorten into winter.
And commercialism's thickening veneer has neither quieted the
cry of every soul, nor stilled its urge to penetrate through it all to
an understanding of this most magnificent event in all creation.

In Holy Scripture whose deep meaning was largely lost by
the fifth century, the wise sage said of God, "He has put eter-
nity into man's mind, yet so that he cannot find out what God
has done from the beginning to the end" (Eccles 3,11). These
words were written during the period of human development
when the splendor of ancient prophecy had faded and the
shades of Sheol, the underworld one experienced at death, were
deepening. It was for humanity truly the "valley of the shadow
of death" and of the "dry bones." In the midst of that valley,
according to Luke, Zechariah, filled with the Holy Spirit,
prophesies that his infant son John shall "give light to those
who sit in … the shadow of death." Yet ere those shades fell,
and even as they were falling, the prophets had spoken of the
days when humanity would rise again to a more divine insight.

And at the very depths of that valley, the valley of human development, there came to a people in pregnant expectancy an event they could only feel, not understand. And so it has been to this very day.

But we are at the time of a new nativity, a time when a new understanding must enter into human evolution. Exploding intellectual development and reliance upon ever increasing materiality is starving the very roots of what we once felt so instinctively. We cannot hope to regain what was lost through mere sentimentality. Those days in our development have passed just as childhood, ever in memory, cannot be reclaimed in advancing age. This reality is built into each of our individual lives, and so is the reality built into human development that it goes from stage to stage. We have reached the time when, according to Paul, we must put away childish speaking, thinking and reasoning and look with maturity on this most important event in human existence.

We are on the threshold of Christianity's adulthood. A clear parallel can be seen between its centuries and the development of an individual human being up to adulthood. For instance, the infancy of the Church up to the time of its recognition as the Roman Catholic Church (roughly 0 to 300) compares to the child who at three years of age recognizes its own identity and begins to say "I play" instead of "Johnny play." From 0 to 700, the period the Church was guided by the Church Fathers, compares to the child until second dentition at seven years of age; from 700 to 1400, the period of the Holy Roman Empire, to later childhood; from 1400 to 2100, to the period of rebellion and conflict within the Church—its period of youth or adolescence; and from 2100 onwards, the flourishing of true Christianity in its adulthood. Christianity's twenty-first century is upon us.

The seed for that adult understanding was sown in the first quarter of our century. But it has lain germinating in its original German language. Only in the last few years has its tender shoot pierced through to any exposure in America. I speak of the spiritual revelations of the Austrian Rudolf Steiner (1861-1925). Characteristic of the truly prophetic, it was not widely recognized in its time or place. Its germinating seed lay hidden until now when, at its right time, it has broken forth in newness of life.

Just as there was no room in the inn for Luke's Jesus child, so also has our scientific, commercial and warlike century had no room for the type of knowledge and wisdom that reveals the deep secrets of the birth of Jesus. In truth, save for an instinctive understanding, now passing away, humanity has not been ready for this knowledge since the day of that holy birth. As Jesus told us in John's Gospel, there were many things that humanity simply was not ready for then. They were to be revealed to it when the time was right, just as some things can come into understanding only as one grows into adulthood.

Christmas Day

While most Christians are vaguely aware that the actual date of Jesus' birth was lost to history, they are not aware of how or when our Christmas day was set on December 25. During the first three centuries of our era, the birth of Christ was celebrated not on that date but on the date of the Epiphany, January 6, in memory of the event when the Spirit of Christ, as the dove, was seen to descend from the heavens and land upon Jesus of Nazareth at his Baptism. Our "twelve days of Christmas" culminate at its threshold. So much is said in the number "twelve" from the Bible's beginning to its end, all buried in the birth of the Jesus child.

It was not until the fourth century when the Emperor Constantine merged Christianity into the Roman political system that December 25 was chosen—chosen because it had long been celebrated by the ancients because of its proximity to the annual birth of the Sun, the winter solstice (equinox) when days began again to lengthen. While Augustine barely remembered it, we no longer comprehend the spiritual reality behind the Sun worship of the ancients and how it related to the sojourn of the descending Christ in the Sun sphere. Nor do we understand how the Earth became the spiritual Sun when Christ's blood dropped into it. Surely the spiritual Sun must have been born on the day the Sun is born each year, December 25. Christian chronographers at that time reckoned the solstices as occurring on the 25th day of March and December (see *16 Encylopaedia Britannica 305*, 1992).

This is but a hint that there is much about the birth of Jesus that is certainly beyond the ribbons and the tinsel, or even the Midnight Mass, insofar as our understanding of this most magnificent event in all of human development is concerned.

Seeming Conflicts and Differences between the Gospel Accounts

In order to understand the depths to which we have sunk in our quest to understand the birth of Jesus, we need to start by looking at how the best of our theological thinking conjures up before our eyes seemingly irreconcilable conflicts between the two birth accounts, Matthew and Luke. (This was, of course, the first essential step that had to be taken.) All recognize some points of similarity, leading naturally to the conclusion that they both tell of the same event, a conclusion never questioned until the commencement of Rudolf Steiner's spiritual disclosures early in the twentieth century. So extensive are these differences and conflicts that serious theologians have uniformly concluded that while one or the other account could be fully historical they cannot both be, likely neither.

One problem that theology has either not recognized, or having recognized has chosen to ignore, has to do with John the Baptist. If, as heretofore assumed, both Nativity accounts describe the same event, then there could have been no John the Baptist, for he would have died when Herod, according to Matthew's Gospel, slew all the infants in the region who were under two years of age, for John was of Judah and only six months older than Jesus according to Luke's Gospel. The existence of this circumstance, so very important, is but one of those many things buried in scripture that were to come to light when the time was right. And one has to wonder how Luke, as thorough as he was in describing the birth of John, could have left unexplained by so much as a single detail how the child escaped such a horrible fate.

Some of the many discrepancies that have been noted between the respective Nativity accounts in the Gospels of Matthew and Luke do not necessarily render the respective accounts incompatible. In other cases, however, the differences are irreconcilable if the two accounts purport to describe the birth of the same child and are both assumed to be completely true.

In addition to the problem of John the Baptist that was mentioned above, let us look at others that have been widely observed. Let us look first at the differences that are clearly inconsistencies.

The genealogies are different in many ways, including:

a) Matthew's genealogy begins his account; Luke's does
   not appear until after Jesus is baptized by John.
b) Matthew goes back to Abraham; Luke goes back to
   Adam as the son of God.
c) Matthew lists forty-two generations from Abraham;
   Luke lists seventy-seven from Adam, with fifty-seven
   of them being from Abraham.
d) Matthew shows the descent through David's son
   Solomon; Luke through David's son, Nathan.
e) As a matter of form rather than substance, Matthew
   narrates from father to son; Luke from son to father.

While several of these differences are not necessarily in conflict, item c) would seem to be, and item d) clearly is (this is
more fully shown in *The Burning Bush*).

In Matthew the parents live in Bethlehem before the conception and birth; in Luke they live in Nazareth.

Matthew places the birth in a house; Luke in a stable with
the infant placed in a manger.

In Matthew's account the journey with the child to Nazareth has to be far later than the return there by the family in
Luke's Gospel.

To the four incompatible differences listed above should be
added the problem of the survival of John the Baptist previously mentioned.

Other differences listed below have been widely noted and,
while not necessarily incompatible on an individual basis,
nevertheless paint a picture of such different circumstances as
to strongly suggest that they do not describe the same event.

In Matthew the announcing angel appears to Joseph; in
Luke it appears to Mary.

In Matthew Joseph is puzzled by his espoused's pregnancy; in Luke he shows no such reaction.

Matthew tells of the visit of the magi and their threefold gifts, Herod's scheme, the angelic warning to Joseph, the flight into and sojourn in Egypt, the angelic direction to return to Israel, and the decision to go to Nazareth in Galilee rather than Bethlehem out of fear regarding Herod's son Archelaus; Luke says nothing of any of this.

Matthew cites five prophetic passages as being fulfilled in his Nativity account; Luke cites none. The last such prophecy, "He shall be called a Nazarene," is not to be found in the canon, suggesting a wider scope of prophecy applicable to this child.

Matthew's Nativity says nothing about John the Baptist; Luke gives an extensive account of the birth of John, the relationship between Mary and Elizabeth, Mary's journey to and sojourn with Elizabeth, the effect of the voice of the impregnated Mary upon the infant in Elizabeth's womb, and the importance of the child being given the name "John."

Matthew says nothing of Mary's inspiration; Luke gives her extensive Magnificat.

Except for the return to Nazareth, Matthew includes none of the enormous panorama of events narrated by Luke's second chapter, including:

a) The enrollment by Caesar Augustus when Quirinius was governor of Syria;
b) The journey from Nazareth to Bethlehem;
c) The enwrapment in swaddling cloths;
d) The appearance of the angel and then the heavenly chorus to the shepherds by night in the field;
e) The visit of the shepherds;
f) The wonderment by Mary and her pondering of these events in her heart;

g) The circumcision of the infant;

h) The purification according to the law of Moses;

i) The presentation of the infant in Jerusalem, and the offering of a sacrifice there;

j) The account of Simeon's vision of his master, his blessing upon the family, and his prophecy to Mary;

k) The account of the prophetess Anna; and

l) Most significantly, the account of the twelve-year old Jesus in the temple.

Both Nativity accounts are part of the Bible, and like the larger whole, can be taken to be literally true if not interpreted as one understands our everyday prose. It clearly incorporates some historical facts, but not for the purpose of telling history. It is telling a spiritual story of the greatest magnitude to which any historical facts utilized are indentured—mere servants of a far larger purpose. The story has served so well during that time of Christendom's infancy, childhood, youth and adolescence. But as the third millennium dawns, a greater maturity of understanding is imperative. It must be seen that allegory, metaphor, poetry, all the literary arsenal, are equally tools to be employed. The important thing in the writing is not whether its account was literally true in the vulgar mode, as mere earthly phenomena, but rather whether it was true in its ultimately more real and lasting spiritual meaning. Ideally and often it was true in both, at least sufficiently so that its earthly connection was clear. But seldom will the deepest meaning be attained through a strictly earthly understanding of the words, for the Evangelists wrote of what they saw with eyes of spirit.

All the major Biblical writers utilized forms other than mere prosaic accounts of historical fact. Jesus especially did this for the uninitiated, for he frequently spoke in parables.

And Paul shows us specifically in Galatians that Moses spoke in allegories. The things they spoke represented spiritual truth, though they intentionally used a story often wholly or partly fictional from the vulgar standpoint to convey the spiritual truth. Preachers today do the same. Too often when the Bible is read it is assumed that the events reflected in the Gospels superseded the application of this principle of interpretation for those of us for whom the Gospels were written. But we delude ourselves if we think that the stories that have come down to us, and the events that took place in them historically, make us any different from the multitudes to whom the parables themselves were given. The Bible is itself a large allegory reflecting deep spiritual reality in which a few beautiful historical facts are also related.

As it happens, there is more historical accuracy in both of the Nativity accounts than our scholars have imagined. It is only since the last part of the nineteenth century, as Christendom enters its late adolescence if you please, that serious question has been widely directed toward all the seeming conflicts in the Nativity accounts. This was a necessary step in the process of the blooming forth of a deeper understanding in maturing Christendom from adolescence into adulthood in the third millennium of its life.

Two Different Lines of Descent

There is no better place for Christians to begin in the always strange but wondrous journey from adolescence into adulthood than with the stories of the birth of Jesus.

And the first thing we must address there is the shocking revelation, almost universally unnoticed, that Matthew clearly tells us Jesus was descended from David's son Solomon while in Luke David's son Nathan was his ancestor. We don't even notice this because the two Gospel genealogies are so different that they are seen in their entireties as merely one of the numerous conflicts causing the accounts to be non-historical. Moreover, as we shall later see, from a historical standpoint each account contains within itself obvious errors based upon Old Testament genealogical information. We don't really bother to read them anymore.

We shall indeed see that while the Evangelists themselves did at least minor doctoring with them to make historical fact serve spiritual revelation, the genealogies are otherwise essentially accurate reflections of the earthly ancestry of Jesus, "who was descended from David according to the flesh" as Paul says in the third Pauline verse of our Bible. In other words, what seem to us to be errors in the genealogical accounts from a historical standpoint are modifications intentionally made by the Evangelists to reflect deeper spiritual realities.

And when we have unraveled this seeming but non-existing conflict we shall also have resolved all the other seeming conflicts and differences between the two Gospel birth accounts, even from a historical point of view (if we can use the word "historical" to also cover what we call "prehistorical").

Seeing, Hearing and Understanding

In his famous "call" chapter, Isaiah tells of speaking with the Christ Spirit after the Seraphim had cleansed his guilty lips. The Lord tells him to tell his people that they will see but not see, hear but not hear, and not understand. Every Gospel, the book of Acts and Paul's letter to the Romans all quote and emphasize this passage. Paul again speaks of it in Hebrews, saying there is "much to say [about Melchizedek] which is hard to explain, since you have become dull of hearing." And Isaiah is told that this condition of darkness will prevail for a long time. It is true, as Isaiah foresaw, that a great light would be seen by the people who dwelt in the deep darkness. But it would be a light so great that it would not be fully comprehended for a time. Christendom has wrongly assumed that the veil was fully pulled back for it at Christ's Resurrection. The veil of the Temple, the human body, was then pulled back, but only as to the body of Christ, who enables it through time for every human soul. Christ came at the depth of humanity's "valley of the shadow of death." And just as one does not enter a long valley precipitously, so also is the journey out not a short, steep one.

Isaiah's prophecy can be understood only by coming to realize that there are two types of seeing and hearing. One relates to our earthly mineral-physical seeing and hearing; the other to a seeing or hearing in the spiritual world. At that point in human evolution that we call "the Fall," there commenced an ever so gradual darkening of human perception of spiritual realities. Clairvoyance and clairaudience were faculties possessed by all who were to become human. Humanity's descent from "the Garden" involved a densification and hardening, and as this proceeded over ages and stages these perceptive faculties faded as the more sensitive human components drew within the mineral-physical body and intelligence increased. Only by these components can we perceive in the spiritual world, and we lose this ability as they become "veiled" by the flesh. In the Bible, over and over again it is referred to as God's "hiding his face." Had Christ not come at just "the right time," hardening would have continued beyond the point of no return. But salvation was made possible for all humanity and indeed for all of creation by the Christ Event.

When it is said that one must become "blind" in order to
see, it means that one must become blind, so to speak, to the
illusory mineral-physical world if one is to see into the spiritual reality that stands behind it. It was primarily in this sense
that Homer was termed "the blind poet." And just as the pro-
gressive development of each of our five senses of the outer
world is reflected in the Biblical account of the Fall, so also
will the human soul develop new organs of perception in its
reascent into the spiritual world from which it came. The
rending of the veil of the Temple by Christ meant the eventual rending of the veil of the mineral-physical body so that
spiritual reality could again be seen, but in a higher, transformed way.

The start toward a more complete understanding of what
lay ahead for humanity had to await two millennia from the
initial unveiling by Christ, for the time would not be right
until then. There is a parabolic symmetry to the descent and
reascent of humanity. The new understanding opened to
humanity at the end of the second millennium is the mirror
image of the accelerating descent into brain thinking that
commenced with Abraham two millennia before Christ. The
story of the Prodigal Son has its highest application as it
reflects the journey of the fallen son, Adam, and the Father's
sacrifice of what belonged by right to the higher Son, Christ.
It applies to every human being in that every soul makes the
entire journey from beginning to end. This is vividly
expressed in the middle of the thirty-eighth chapter of Job,
when the message of the book of Job becomes clear. We shall
come back to Job in a little while, but for now the following
portions of the chapter should give us a clear hint of this reality (my emphasis):

Then the Lord answered Job out of the whirlwind: ...
"Where were you when I laid the foundation of the earth
... when the morning stars sang together, and all the
sons of God shouted for joy? ... Have the gates of death
been revealed to you ... ? ... Where is the way to the
dwelling of light, and where is the place of darkness, that
you may take it to its territory and that you may discern
the paths to its home? *You know, for you were born then,
and the number of your days is great!*"

The book of Job is the story of humanity, but in order to
have meaning for any human being it is also at the same time
the story of every human being. It is meaningless otherwise.
Neither Christ nor the Psalmist could have referred to us as
"gods" if it were not so. Each of us was born ages ago before
the gates of death began dimming our spiritual consciousness
with the Fall and the tree of life began to be replaced by the
tree of knowledge. Before the Fall, our consciousness extended
to spiritual beings and was continuous. Death was unknown.
Death began to develop with the Fall, so that our consciousness was interrupted—but only our consciousness, not our
essential being. And over long ages the spiritual beings progressively "hid their face" as the Bible tells us over and over.

As the wise sage said, "There is no remembrance of former
things," and for that reason do we eat, drink and make merry.

If Christendom is to be able to comprehend the Bible's
deeper meaning, it must jettison some concepts and open its
mind to others, else the revelation cannot come. It will con-
tinue to see and hear in an earthly and material way but not
see, hear or understand in a spiritual way. One can see a close
parallel between the way the ecclesiastic authority interpreted
scripture in the day of Christ and the way it interprets it today.

This is always a danger when the frozen written word prevails over true intuitive prophecy. In ancient time there was no need for writing, and the major prophets, relied upon by Paul, have told us that this day must come again. The Bible is sacred, and is literally true, but only if it can be understood in its deeper prophetic sense. The day for understanding it otherwise is past. Our times are demanding new comprehension.

Two Critical Concepts

It is my conviction, after a lifetime of studying and teaching the Bible from a traditional Christian perspective and then opening my mind and heart to Steiner's amazing intuitions, that neither the Nativity nor the Bible can be truly understood unless two concepts new to Christendom are taken by it to heart. The one who cannot look at these as at least being possible will profit little from reading on. The first necessity is to comprehend the true structure of every human being, and the second is to realize that human souls reincarnate. What the Bible calls "destiny," and in the Orient is called "karma," is a spiritual reality. The first of these necessary concepts is new to Christian theology. The second, when not rejected outright, has been consensually ignored. But Christendom is presented in our time with the essential cornerstone that its builders have thus far either rejected or overlooked.

Both of these concepts are fully elaborated and Biblically documented in my longer work, *The Burning Bush*. Even the passage in Hebrews, "... it is appointed for men to die once, and after that comes judgment," seemingly so devastating to the idea of reincarnation, is not contrary to it. In truth, it can be seen in my longer work to be even more essential to the reality of reincarnation than to its attempted refutation. That will become crystal clear when the function of the "judgment" it mentions and the distinction between "the judgment of the Father" and "the judgment of the Son" is understood. In this shorter version we can touch upon each of these two essential concepts but lightly.

Existing prejudice, especially in the more conservative mind, will doubtless focus upon the second of these concepts, reincarnation and its related karma. It was almost precisely at the time when modern Bible commentaries began to be written (one Alfred Edersheim published his landmark commentary in 1883) that H. P. Blavatsky began to reveal the Oriental perspectives of reincarnation in the West. Since that time, most of what has been written and said about reincarnation outside of anthroposophical circles must be taken as false and misleading, for reasons set out in *The Burning Bush*. We must leave for that larger work the extensive showing that the Bible has buried deep within its hold, and thus eventually mandates the acceptance of, the spiritual reality that the human soul, though not its bodies or earthly personalities, lives again and again, purified between lives by the "refiner's fire" that burns away its dross. Only through this process of being born again and again can it attain to the eventual perfection required to fully return to its heavenly home. Only then does it not have to "die any more," as Jesus says to the Sadducees in Luke's Gospel. To Moses (as Jesus clearly implies in his answer to the Sadducees) it was the burning bush that is not consumed. To Isaiah it was the oak or terebinth whose stump was burned again and again but still retained its vitality to grow. It is of a shoot from just such a stump of the root of Jesse that the Gospels, especially Matthew, speak.

We mistakenly assume that the idea of reincarnation came only from the Orient, for it existed also earlier in the West.

We have only to look to Plato, and then to the pre-existence of the soul in Origen's work. It is simply that the destiny of the West was to delve more deeply into the development of the intellect, overshooting if you will in that direction, forgetting for a time its former knowledge, while the Orient stayed temporarily behind with its fading ancient traditions. Christ walked the Earth between East and West, and the time has arrived when our knowledge of his mission must come to fruition in order that East and West shall again become one.

We must see in the Blavatsky phenomenon merely one of the early stirrings of the divine intelligence, the first rifts in the cocoon of hidden Biblical truths, as the right time for new revelations began to dawn, when human beings would be ready for them. What then came forth from Steiner as seed must break forth with the dawning of the third millennium.

We cannot hope to even begin to understand the mystery of the Nativity until we learn something about the true nature of the human being. Our thoughts immediately turn to matters of physiology and what one might expect to learn in medical training. But thus far this training, as we know it today, deals only with the physically perceptible body. Even in its explorations into the mind it has been unable to progress much beyond that point.

Steiner has shown us, and the Bible extensively confirms, that the human "body" is threefold, composed really of three distinct bodies, the respective seeds for which were laid in three successive primeval "Conditions of Consciousness" before Earth evolution even began. Abraham brought with him from Ur (the word *Ur* itself has to do with origins or prototypes) at least some vague understanding of these, and they became the source of the names of the first three days of the ancient week, Saturday, Sunday and Monday (see *12*

Encyclopaedia Britannica 555, 1992, under "week"). Earth evolution is the fourth such Condition of Consciousness, and three more will follow it before the end of the sevenfold Conditions when creation will fully return to its heavenly origin. (One might see in the Four Worlds of the Hopi Indian legend something of this ancient insight.)

The three "kingdoms" below humanity, the Mineral Kingdom, Plant Kingdom and Animal Kingdom, are made up of what we might call the beings that fell behind during these first three Conditions so as to be servants of the highest kingdom on Earth, the Human Kingdom. The human being is not descended from any of these. Rather these are the by-products, so to speak, of the Human Kingdom, representing those that fell behind to progressively greater or lesser extent during the earlier Conditions. The human being has in it something of each of these lower kingdoms, but these lower elements must be overcome in the last three Conditions, during which creation will also be redeemed.

The human being's three bodies are the physical body, the etheric body and the astral body. The physical is the form for mineral accumulation. The etheric is also called the life body, and is what gives life and healing. The astral body is the consciousness body. Our senses are the tools of the astral body which is the seat of all passions, desires, pain, joy, thinking, and the like. Our deeper feelings and more permanent disposition stem more from the etheric body. These characterizations are extremely abbreviated, but they are like the "a-b-c's," essential to learn at the beginning and challenging in application throughout life. Their relationship to each other may be compared with the relationship of the clock's hour hand (physical), minute hand (etheric) and second hand (astral). The human Ego, also called the "I Am," the mind, or the soul, has direct control only over the astral body during Earth evolution. Its influence over the lower bodies is then like that of the second hand upon the minute hand and then the hour hand in turn. As essential as a growing understanding of these bodies is, it is beyond the scope of this shorter work to go into them in any greater detail. They are mentioned here only to permit some comprehension of the Nativity accounts. Unless they are conditionally accepted, these accounts can be neither clarified nor meaningfully reconciled.

A knowledge of these bodies is also essential if countless other portions of the Bible are to come into our fuller understanding. For instance, the one verse parable in the thirteenth chapter of Matthew about "the kingdom of heaven [being] like leaven which a woman took and hid in three measures of flour till it was all leavened" reflects this threefold reality. The Ego that sets the Human Kingdom apart from the Animal Kingdom is the leaven (when the higher Christ "I Am" is taken into it) that must eventually spiritualize the three bodies into their three higher spiritual counterparts. The first of these three higher parts is called *manas* in the Orient, which is the same as the Biblical "manna." When all is done, heaven is attained.

Luke's version of this is given in the three verses that tell about a friend on a journey who arrives at the midnight hour seeking "three loaves," which are "loaned" to him for his further journey. Our three bodies are indeed "loaned" to us in a sense, for they do not move from one life to another. Only the journeying soul does that. It is like both Cain and Job, wandering on, suffering but unable itself to die.

A more complete example is the entire book of Job. Until the three friends are seen as the three bodies, and Elihu as the entry of the soul (Ego or "I Am"), the "youngest" of the group, the book cannot be understood, even as an explanation for why the innocent must suffer. But when seen in this anthroposophical light, then the understanding becomes complete. Job is, after all, simply a longer version of the journey of the Prodigal Son reflected both in Luke's Gospel and in the Bible as an entirety.

It is well to know that we speak of the eternal soul or Ego that is burned but not destroyed as an "Individuality." It is "the burning bush that is not consumed." The "Personality," on the other hand, is the manifestation of an Individuality in a particular earthly lifetime. With our senses, we perceive today only the Personality. The day will come when we, along with the initiates, will be able to perceive the Individuality. For some this may not be far away.

Two Common Features

Now let us consider two things common to both Nativity accounts (there are others, of course).

First, they both trace Jesus' ancestry through the blood of his father, Joseph. Only Steiner has explained to us the great mystery of how Jesus could actually have been born of the earthly seed of Joseph, otherwise so thoroughly hidden by the Gospel accounts, while at the same time having been born of the virgin Mary. And in this respect, we need not understand the term "virgin" to mean merely "a young woman," as it can be properly interpreted by translation.

Second, both accounts clearly contain what have heretofore been seen to be errors in genealogical listing. But they are erroneous only if understood merely as indicating history. While they clearly intend to show blood descent through Joseph as the natural earthly father, they have a deeper spiritual purpose in mind in their obviously intentional manipulation of the number of generations.

Matthew stresses the number forty-two, while Luke lists seventy-seven. We shall see the immense and respective significance of these. In order to get to his number forty-two, Matthew leaves out of his middle group of fourteen generations three successive Judean kings (Ahaziah, Joash and Amajiah) between Joram and Uzziah. It would have been virtually impossible for one such as Matthew to have missed these, for they were etched deeply into the history of the Hebrew people. Their intentional omission, in order to be able to come to three groupings of fourteen each, must surely be a significant message to later times.

Luke, on the other hand, adds at least one name to his list in order to get a total of seventy-seven. Except for that, both Gospels list fourteen names from Abraham through David. Luke, however, takes the one Matthew calls "Ram" and makes of him the two ancestors called "Arni" and "Admin." Old Testament accounts (Ruth and Chronicles) support Matthew's list on this discrepancy.

The Solomon Jesus Child of Matthew's Gospel

With this, let us look first at the birth in Matthew's Gospel. Steiner calls the child there "Solomon Jesus," because its ancestry is through David's son Solomon.

The lineage of the Matthew child is traced through forty-two generations from Abraham to Jesus. These are carefully divided into three groups of fourteen generations each. The deep wisdom involved in this arrangement came from a prehistoric Zarathustra of ancient Persia, about 5,000 B.C., who had seen the descending Christ in the Sun's aura. This wisdom was preserved in the ancient mystery schools. Finally it came through the esoteric instruction of the Essenes' "True Teacher," Jeschu ben Pandira, about 100 B.C., who taught how it was necessary to perfect what had been given to Abraham in its first rudiments so that a threefold human body would be able to receive the highly advanced human Ego of Zarathustra, who would later sacrifice himself to the entry of the great Sun Spirit, the Christ. To receive Zarathustra, it was necessary that there be three successive cycles of fourteen generations to perfect through heredity first the physical, then the etheric and finally the astral body.

Steiner tells us that heredity works in such a way that the qualities transmitted do not pass from one human being to its nearest descendant in the immediately following generation; the salient qualities and attributes cannot be transmitted directly from father to son, from mother to daughter, but only from father to grandson—thus to the second generation, then the fourth, and so on. Thus, fourteen generations were necessary to have seven hereditary steps for the perfection of each of the three bodies. The physical body was perfected in the first fourteen generations, the etheric in the second, and the astral in the third.

The Individuality (Ego or soul) of the great Zarathustra was intimately involved in the preparation of the Solomon Jesus child. In Ancient Persia, Zarathustra had given a precious gift to humanity. This most precious gift was knowledge of the outer world, of the mysteries of the Cosmos received into the human astral body in thinking, feeling and willing. Zarathustra had imparted this mighty truth to his pupils, particularly to the two among them who can be said to have been his most intimate disciples and were incarnated later on as Hermes (founder of the Egyptian culture) and Moses. (Much more is said about this in *The Burning Bush.*) The Zarathustra Individuality continued to develop through successive incarnations, and it could be said that he was the one who above all others had seen most clearly and deeply into the spirituality of the Macrocosm. And with the birth of the Matthew Jesus child, it was time for Zarathustra's great gift to be given again to humanity, in a rejuvenated form. To this end, the Zarathustra Individuality reincarnated, for a time, in the prepared physical body of the Solomon Jesus child of the kingly line, such line being significant because it has to do with knowledge of the outer world.

The name Zarathustra, later also known as Zoroaster (or Nazarathos), means the great lustrous or shining star. Not only is the etheric body, reflecting the human head and four limbs, shaped like a star, but in Zarathustra's case, he was the one who had seen the Ahura Mazdao (the Great Aura), or Christ, sojourning in the Sun, had predicted his future Incarnation on Earth, and was thus himself, as the ultimate vehicle of the Christ, also known by a similar name. The knowledge of all of this existed in those initiated from the time of Zarathustra, and these were known as Magi, or kings by virtue of the magical nature of their abilities in regard to ruling humanity (recalling that the authorities in all fields were the initiated priests in ancient times). These initiates were able to see in the etheric world the descent of their master, Zarathustra, into incarnation in Bethlehem, and this is the "star" that brought them there.

And so we see the immense significance of Matthew's genealogy as an essential part of the Nativity account. But one further point seems critical if we are to appreciate certain things about Matthew's Gospel. Regarding this Gospel, Steiner speaks again of Jeschu ben Pandira as the great

Teacher of the Essenes. This teacher had five pupils each of whom took over a special branch of his general teaching. The names of these five pupils were: Mathai, Nakai, Netzer, Boni and Thona. Jeschu himself suffered martyrdom on account of alleged blasphemy and heresy, a hundred years B.C., but these five propagated his teachings in five different sections. The teaching reflected in Matthew's genealogy was propagated especially by Mathai, and it is from his name that the title of this Gospel derives.

On the other hand, the special concern of the pupil Netzer was the founding of a little colony which led a secluded existence and which then in the Bible received the name "Nazareth." There in Nazareth—Netzereth—an Essene colony was established for those whose lives were dedicated to the ancient Nazirite order who lived here in fairly strict seclusion. Hence after the flight to Egypt and the return, nothing was more natural than that the Jesus of Matthew's Gospel should be brought into the atmosphere of Netzerism. It was for this reason that Matthew spoke of the prophecy being fulfilled to the effect that "He shall be called a Nazarene." No such prophecy exists in the Old Testament. The Evangelist must surely then have considered Jeschu ben Pandira to have been a prophet, and have aimed his Gospel at the Essenes themselves. The Essenic connections of Matthew's Gospel have been seen also by non-anthroposophical writers in recent times.

This then is the background for understanding the significance of the three appearances of the angel to Joseph to announce, *first*, the marvelous spiritual happenings that he was to implement by fathering Zarathustra's incarnation in the Solomon Jesus child, whose conception was thus also by virtue of the Holy Virgin (Sophia, Divine Wisdom) in the spiritual world; *second*, the flight into Egypt; and *third*, the return to Nazareth. We will return later to the question of the virginity of the two Marys and the bewilderment that this caused the Solomon Joseph.

The Nathan Jesus Child of Luke's Gospel

Even more mysterious than the birth of the Solomon Jesus child is the birth of the tender infant in Luke's Gospel, called the "Nathan Jesus" because his earthly ancestry is traced to Joseph through David's son Nathan. The full account of the birth of this child is even more complex than that of the Solomon Jesus child. And it cannot be told without first looking at the evolution of the Earth and of the human being—for the majesty of that child cannot be comprehended without it. Only a brief summary of that evolution can be given here. This evolution is presented in the first three chapters of Genesis, when they are rightly understood, for the birth of this child goes back that far. My longer work, and those of Steiner upon which it is based, go into greater detail.

Steiner held that the Incarnation of Christ represented the fulfillment of all "true religions." The three main streams he identifies as having come to a culminating point through the Incarnation of Jesus Christ are those of Zarathustra, Abraham and Buddha. Previously only the stream of Abraham was recognized, but Steiner shows us that these other streams were also involved, and subsequent discoveries in this century of ancient documents providentially hidden for millennia have confirmed it. We have seen the Zarathustra stream in relation to the Solomon Jesus child. Let us now look at the Buddha stream in the Nathan Jesus child.

Before incarnating the Christ Spirit had to descend from the highest ramparts of the all-encompassing heaven. We can best think of this pervasive Spirit, before its long descent, as having encompassed the vast reaches of our universe to the very edge of nothingness. We are speaking of no tangible body that would have descended in a linear fashion such as we ourselves might do in a spaceship. Rather we must conceive of the vast Christ Spirit as having been spherical, so that its "descent" was brought about by a painful contraction into and through ever smaller spheres.

As is shown in *The Burning Bush*, our own solar system came into being in a somewhat similar manner. In Romans Paul describes the spiritual pain involved in such a contraction, saying "that the whole creation has been groaning in travail until now." For as Steiner has shown us our entire solar system came into its earliest existence as a mere fireball. But nothing had condensed so far as to yet constitute molecular heat as we know it. Rather it was spiritual heat, of the same nature as what Moses called the Spirit of God moving over the face of the waters. It is related to what causes our physical body to maintain its internal temperature independent of its surroundings. Genesis thus opens its account with three non-tangible formless elements, water, air and fire. These, in their etheric nature, or in "their kind" as Genesis says, were the products of the three Conditions of Consciousness from which we name our Saturday, Sunday and Monday. The Genesis account of creation thus does not go back so far as does the Prologue of St. John's Gospel. The Christ-enabled vision of John saw further in both directions, backward and forward, than the more limited vision of Moses.

This vast fireball was brought into existence by the activity of the highest Hierarchy, composed of the Seraphim, the Cherubim and the Thrones, as agents of the Christ, the Word of God. Two lower threefold Hierarchies were also involved in the further condensations that brought about our present existence. Esoteric Christian terminology used by Paul names these, and was reduced to writing in the sixth century by Pseudo-Dionysius, who wrote in the name and tradition of Paul's Athenian convert, Dionysius the Areopagite. Thus Paul speaks of Dominions, Powers, Authorities, and Principalities, as well as Archangels and angels, and of Christ as being above all these "names." These are among the "Heavenly Host," and are all involved in the creative process. A remnant of this knowledge existed within Christendom until the sixteenth century when our dedication to the physical world squeezed it out of our acceptable worldly thinking.

The order in which the seven visible bodies of our solar system separated out, along with the Earth, from this condensing original fireball of our solar system is given in *The Burning Bush* as Steiner gave them to us. The seven bodies have long been called the "seven stars" (Rev 1,16,20; 2,1; 3,1) while those in the outer firmament have been called "fixed stars." It is important to understand what all these heavenly bodies represent. Each one is the materially visible body of spiritual beings. Just as our mineral-physical body is only the outer manifestation of our soul and spirit, so also is every tangible thing, both on Earth and in the heavens, merely the concrete manifestation or evidence of some spiritual being or group of beings.

Those spiritual beings, for instance, who have our Sun for their home, actually occupy what we call the Sun sphere, that spherical realm defined by the orbit of the Sun as though it revolved around the Earth—at least this is the sphere's definition since the Earth became the spiritual Sun when Christ descended from the Sun to the Earth.

The spiritual beings who have the Sun sphere for their home are the ones whom the Bible calls the *Elohim*. This is the Hebrew term for the seven spiritual beings called God in the first Chapter of Genesis. Their plurality has befuddled later Christianity which tends to think of God as one. But it was not so in Genesis one. The Greek word for these beings is *Exusiai*, and it is translated into English as the "Authorities." An inspection of the Greek New Testament will disclose this.

The original fireball actually was the manifestation of a large number of active spiritual beings at multiple stages of development. What was needed for the further development of a given level of beings was different from that needed by all the other levels, so that there were successive separations in the evolution of our solar system. The first to separate out was Saturn, then Jupiter, for beings too retarded to condense further with the rest. Next came the Sun for those more advanced, and they took with them all except what were to become Earth and Moon. Mars then separated from the Sun, passing through the Earth into its outer orbit, and depositing in Earth what later developed into iron, a necessary component of human blood. Obviously, for this latter to have happened, the vast rarified and fluid spherical condition of each of them had to be far different than their present materialized form—as it was. Recent discoveries, however, thought to evidence primeval cellular existence on Mars as well as the planet's former fluid condition and thicker atmosphere, may well be explained by this event put forward long ago by Steiner.

At this point it was necessary for further human development that the lower spiritual beings in the Earth-Moon mass be separated out. This happened in the separation of the Moon from the Earth, leaving the Earth as it now is. Still later, Archangels who were less advanced than the Elohim, separated out from the Sun-Venus-Mercury mass into Venus and Mercury, leaving only the Elohim as the Sun Beings.

However, when the Moon separated from the Earth, the most exalted one of the Elohim sacrificed its higher state and went to the Moon (the Moon sphere, compressed more closely to Earth than any other) in order from that vantage point to work more closely with human development on the Earth. Though it occupied the Moon sphere along with beings lower than earthly humans, it was too high to descend into the Earth sphere itself, nor could it have carried out its mission by doing so. This particular Eloha is the one called Yahweh. Yahweh became the "one God" of the Hebrew people, the source of its Shema. In the sixth chapter of Deuteronomy we thus read, "Hear, O Israel: The Lord our God is one Lord." And the Hebrew people thus took for themselves a calendar based upon the Moon rather than the Sun.

But from the Moon, Yahweh truly reflected the light of Christ who had by now descended (condensed) into the Sun sphere. Christ could now speak to human souls through Yahweh, and so he did.

All evolution within our solar system takes place in a sevenfold manner. The sage Solomon tells us, "Wisdom [Sophia] has built her house, she has set up her seven pillars" (Prov 9,1). All is fractal in nature so that the largest sevenfold existence is divided and subdivided again and again in sevenfold units. Earth evolution is the fourth Condition of Consciousness, following ancient Saturn, Sun and Moon (the earlier-mentioned ancient conditions from which our Saturday, i.e., Saturn's day, Sunday and Monday were named). Earth evolution itself is divided by the part before Christ and the part after. Two more conditions of consciousness will follow Earth evolution. Then is creation in the kingdom of heaven—all three loaves (the three bodies) are then fully leavened, as the parables in Matthew and Luke suggest. All seven of these conditions of consciousness are reflected in the names of the days of our week, as shown in *The Burning Bush*.

The first three verses of Genesis reflect the third epoch of Earth evolution, called Lemuria, when the etheric (formless and non-tangible) elements of water, air and fire already existed as a result of the recapitulation, in the Earth's first three epochs, of the spiritual developments in the first three conditions of consciousness. The fourth such epoch is called Atlantis, the ancient continent that sank into what became the Atlantic Ocean during the late ice ages. The Biblical account of Noah tells of those who came over into our fifth epoch, called the post-Atantean. The first two Cultural Eras of our post-Atlantean epoch, those of ancient India and ancient Persia, are prehistoric. Writing and recorded history begins in the third Cultural Era, called the Chaldo-Egyptian.

In his descent from the highest heaven, the Christ Spirit became the leader of those spiritual beings on the Sun who previously had caused the Sun to separate from the Earth in the second epoch of Earth evolution. John, in the prologue of his Gospel, speaks of "the fullness" of Christ. Steiner tells us that by this "fullness" he means the light of all seven Elohim, not just of Yahweh alone.

In the second Cultural Era Zarathustra, as we have seen, saw Christ in the Sun's aura, calling him the Great Aura, or Ahura Mazdao, or Ormuzd. And humanity worshiped the Sun in that era and the next. As time went on and Christ approached ever nearer the Earth, Moses saw him in the burning bush and called him Yahweh-Eloha. Even later the Christ Spirit brought one Siddhartha Gautama to enlightenment under the bodhi tree as the great Buddha.

Here Steiner says, "This question brings us to the threshold of one of the greatest mysteries of Earth evolution," one difficult for people today to have any inkling of.

The mission of the one who became Gautama Buddha (6th century B.C.) was to incorporate into humanity the principle of compassion and love, for nowhere prior to this did it exist in humanity. Love prior to that time was related to the blood. Even later on, Christ had to illustrate that the Levitical commandment to "love one's neighbor as oneself" included persons of mixed Jewish blood, leaving aside for then those wholly Gentile. Conscience sprang from this very Buddhistic insight. Buddha's Eightfold Path endowed humanity with something completely new in human relationships—but it was totally Christ inspired. Until then, morality was introduced through revelations given from without, as in the Ten Commandments. Such inwardness as the Buddha revealed had to be withheld from the Hebrew people until the right time. Until then, the external "law" had to prevail. Paul speaks of this comparative phenomenon in the second chapter of Romans.

We have sketched above something of the evolution of our Earth in order now to look at the parallel evolution of the human being. The seeds of the three bodies of the human being, the physical, etheric and astral, trace their origins respectively to the three ancient Conditions of Consciousness. These three were then recapitulated in the first three Epochs of the Earth Condition of Consciousness, so that they alone composed the human condition at the time when, in Genesis Two, Yahweh appears on the separated Moon. As yet the human Ego (its "I Am") had not penetrated into any of these bodies. Nor had the androgynous human being yet separated into male and female. As the Bible tells us, this took place in the developments leading up to and included in the account of the Fall.

It is at this point that an event took place in the spiritual world of such importance that the Nativity account in Luke's Gospel simply cannot be understood without it.

The account of the Fall of humanity from the Garden is the story of the infection of the human astral body, the sense body of appetite and desire, the one that deals with all animalistic consciousness. As yet the "I Am" had not entered. It only enters after the astral body has been infected by the fruit of the "tree of knowledge." Only then do Adam and Eve speak in the first person as "I." This came about because of the ungodly desire to descend into mineral existence. Over time the creating gods could see that the infection of the astral body would lead to the consequential infection of the etheric and physical bodies, and to their earthly pain, toil and death. As Paul said, all of his "members" were pervaded by this infection ("For I delight in the law of God, in my inmost self, but I see in my members another law at war with the law of my mind and making me captive to the law of sin which dwells in my members"). So prior to, or contemporaneous with, the separation of the human into male and female, these powers held back from it a portion of its etheric nature or body. The etheric body is also known as the "life" body. It is this retention that Moses calls the separation of the "tree of life." It is seen also in the second chapter of Job, before God permits Satan access to Job; this reflects the account of Cain (who could not die) immediately following the separation of the "tree of life." These accounts are so important because they are archetypal for every human being.

What I have just explained is the basis for understanding what Paul calls "the first and second Adam." The etheric (life) body that went into Adam and Eve is what Paul calls "the first Adam." The etheric body held back from Adam by the creating powers is what Paul calls "the second Adam." The sexual nature of the human being's etheric body is opposite that of its physical. Thus the male has a female etheric body, and conversely the female a male etheric body. Perhaps this helps explain why one yearns for the other. Their "desire" is for each other, as is said of Adam and Eve.

The virginal female etheric body withheld from Adam entered into the Nathan Jesus child of Luke's Gospel, and the unspoiled male etheric body withheld from Eve entered into the Mary of that Gospel. Thus both the fetus and the madonna in that Gospel are called "blessed" by Elizabeth. And this phenomenon also explains why the six-month old fetus in Elizabeth's womb leaped for joy at the approach of Mary. For the soul of Adam had reincarnated in Elijah and then, as Luke says, in John the Baptist. And the etheric body of the infant in Mary's womb was the unspoiled mate of the infected etheric body in Elizabeth's womb. So powerful was the divinely pure etheric body in the Nathan Jesus child that it could also serve as a provisional Ego for that child until it was twelve years old, for it was to be a vehicle for the Christ and the Christ "I Am" had never yet dwelt within a human body.

Only two of the New Testament writers, or of the Apostles, were fully initiated by the Christ. One of these was the Evangelist John, clearly identified in *The Burning Bush*. The other was Paul who was initiated into the highest mysteries in his Damascus Road experience. Evangelist John's writings were the deeper, for Paul's mission was different, though in Hebrews he was able to set forth deeper spiritual truths more systematically, which accounts for its much different nature. Still in Paul's other letters there flash forth, from time to time, things that have not yet been understood but that show clearly the depth of his insight when understood in anthroposophical light.

And one of these insights is his expressed knowledge of the first and second Adam. Paul's tutorship of Luke is well known, and we may take it that the latter was himself initiated by Paul, an "eyewitness" in the spiritual world and servant of the Word, so that he could write such a magnificent Gospel of insight.

So the Nathan Jesus child can be seen to have the unspoiled etheric body withheld before the Fall as both his etheric body and provisional Ego. And Luke shows us that the physical body of this child descended, according to the flesh, through Joseph. We shall deal with this and its relationship to Mary's virginity after looking at the source of the child's astral body.

This is where the Buddha enters. The Buddha, though no longer required to incarnate, continued to work with humanity from the spiritual world. He continued to work down as far as the astral and etheric worlds. Steiner tells us that it was the image of the glorified astral body of Buddha, he who had first brought into humanity's evolution the principle of peace and goodwill, that appeared, along with the angel, as the heavenly host, to the shepherds; likewise in the radiance that surrounded the Nathan Jesus child before the shepherds in the manger. But the Buddha played a far larger role in the Nativity of this child.

Only reverently can we now approach the event of the birth of the Nathan Jesus child to the very young Mary, barely into childbearing age. The soul of the Nathan Mary, which received the portion of Eve's etheric body held back by the divine powers and not affected by the Fall, had not gone through prior incarnations, and was thus virginal. It had not built up any instinctive consciousness or even awareness of the normal human procreative function. Metaphorically she was an Eve who never ate of the apple, hence could not perceive her nakedness.

So Nathan Mary could not have perceived the occurrence of the procreative act in the same manner as a normal person whose etheric and physical bodies bear the full effect of the Fall, and her soul would have remained virginal thereafter. She knew not any relationship with her husband in the normal sense—whether or not any had occurred. Therefore, her etheric body could not carry the impress of such knowledge and so, the etheric body being what molds the physical, her physical body remained (or resumed its status as) virginal also. She remained pure after conception of the Nathan Jesus child to the time of her death. The six siblings of Jesus (four brothers and two sisters as Mark tells us) were born to the Solomon Mary. Steiner could thus properly refer to the Nathan Mary as the true virgin of the two Marys, though the physical blood of her son was of the line of David through Joseph.

While these deeper insights have long been lost to Roman Catholic theologians, they nevertheless explain why there is validity to their doctrine of the Immaculate Conception and Perpetual Virginity of Mary. Nathan Mary's etheric body, not having gone through the Fall, was immaculate at the very time it was itself conceived and it remained immaculate through her conception of the equally immaculate "Second Adam," the Nathan Jesus child, and thereafter until her early death.

Luke reflects the ages of the souls of the "two Adams" through the ages of their parents, it being necessary that the "old soul" of the "first Adam" should be born of the old parents, Zechariah and Elizabeth, and that the "young soul" of the "second Adam" should be born of the youngest possible parents at the bare threshold of reproductive maturity. The Greek word *parthenon*, translated "virgin," or "Virgo," also means "young woman."

Luke reveals the presence of the purified astral body of Buddha as the astral body of the Nathan Jesus child in the account of Simeon. In one of his lectures, Steiner reveals the nature of this account as follows:

> At the birth of the Nazareth Jesus-Boy there descended into his astral body what we might call the later embodiment of Buddha. Buddha, in his etheric body, was now in this re-embodiment united at birth with the Nazareth Jesus-Boy, so that in the aura of this boy we see Buddha in the astral body. This is very profoundly hinted at in St. Luke's Gospel. The Indian legend related that at the time when Prince Gautama was born, who was to become the Buddha, there lived a wonderful Wise Man, whose name was Asita. Through his clairvoyant faculties he knew that the Bodhisattva had been born. He saw the child in the King's palace, and was filled with enthusiasm. He began to weep. "Why weepest thou," asked the King, "I see no misfortune." "Oh, King, on the contrary, the child now born is the Bodhisattva, and will become the Buddha. I weep because I am an old man and cannot hope to live to see this Buddha." Then Asita died, and the Bodhisattva became the Buddha. Now the Buddha descends from on high and unites himself with the aura of the Nazareth-Jesus-Boy, in order to contribute his mite to the Great Event of Palestine. Through a karmic connection the old Asita was reborn at about the same time, and became Simeon, who now saw the Buddha who from a Bodhisattva had become what he now was. The Bodhisattva as Buddha, whom 600 years before he had not been able to

see, he saw now; for, as he held the Nazareth Jesus-child in his arms, he saw the Buddha soaring above in the child's aura, and he then uttered the beautiful words: "Lord, now lettest thou thy servant depart in peace, for I have seen my Master."

In 1986 my wife and I traveled to Singapore, Hong Kong and China. In one of those locations, I acquired a book on Buddhism. It was given to me free of charge by Bukkyo Dendo Kyokai, of Tokyo, Japan, entitled, *The Teaching of Buddha*, 14th Ed., Tokyo, 1981. The following paragraph about the newborn infant Siddhartha Gautama is found in its introductory biographical sketch:

> A hermit, called Asita, who lived in the mountains not far away, noticed a radiance about the castle and, interpreting it as a good omen, came down to the palace and was shown the child. He predicted: "This Prince, if he remains in the palace, when grown up, will become a great king and subjugate the whole world. But if he forsakes the court life to embrace a religious life, he will become a Buddha, the Savior of the world."

I have also found this legend confirmed in authoritative, secular American writings about Buddhism.

What is meant by saying that this child had in it the Adam soul as it was before the Fall? It means that we are dealing with a soul that had had none of the earthly experiences of humanity, no sophistication whatsoever, no developed aptitude for anything that the culture of humanity had developed over the millennia, no inclination to learning of the type taught to children in schools—the ultimate innocent and naive creature, but with bottomless understanding, compassion and love for all of

God's creatures, an openness to all, an inscrutable power for distinguishing between good and evil, and a primeval understanding of the tree of life withdrawn from the rest of humanity.

This is in contrast to the Solomon Jesus child that embodied the most advanced Ego that human culture had produced, the ancient Zarathustra. We are now ready to consider the one called Jesus of Nazareth.

How the Solomon Jesus and Nathan Jesus Became One

It is clear that before the birth of their Jesus child, the Nathan parents lived in Nazareth and the Solomon parents lived in Bethlehem. When the Solomon family returned from Egypt, they went as the angel had instructed Joseph into Galilee and settled in Nazareth. As one might expect in a small community, they were friendly and the children grew up as neighbors until the Luke child was twelve years of age.[1]

Steiner tells us that the Solomon child was born long enough before the Nathan child to permit John the Baptist to escape the Herod massacre of male children under two years of age. Since John was six months older than the Nathan Jesus, we may assume that the Solomon child was born more than six months before the Nathan child. Those who have studied the matter carefully know that most scholars place the birth of Jesus earlier than our calendar date but that there is a discrepancy of a few years between the proposed dates. Herod the Great's death in 4 B.C. pretty well establishes the birth of

---

1. An article in Lubbock's paper dated December 23, 1997 reports that American Bible scholar and archaeologist Stephen Pfann finds Nazareth to have been "tiny, with two or three clans (of up to 300 people) living in 35 homes spread over six acres."

the Solomon Jesus at least four years B.C., while from the standpoint of Luke's Gospel a date as late as 1 B.C. is suggested. These discussions are beyond the scope of this brief work, but fit the scenario presented.

When the Nathan Jesus child was twelve, an event occurred that had been prepared in the spiritual world over many centuries. It was likely foreseen in the account that reflected the proverbial wisdom of the ancestral Solomon. I speak of the occasion where each of two prostitutes gave birth to a son, one of whom died, whereupon both women claimed the surviving child. Solomon proposed to cut the child in two with a sword and give half to each one, whereupon the real mother immediately gave up her claim so that the child could live. The wise Solomon then pronounced judgment in her favor.

As is so often the case in scripture, the "sword" can mean the mighty Word of God. And we find the wise Simeon telling Nathan Mary that in regard to her infant "a sword will pierce through your own soul also." As events were to unfold, this can be seen to have truly happened in a most profound way.

Believing it important to know what happened between the birth of Jesus and his ministry, scholars of the last century and a half have bemoaned the inadequacy of the Gospels in giving us only the account in Luke's Gospel of the twelve year old Jesus in the temple. But the Gospels have given us all that is really important. And except for the divine spiritual intuition of Rudolf Steiner we would even yet not be able to see its immense significance. What then are we told by him that makes it so significant?

At the time of the Presentation at the Temple the Ego of the Solomon Jesus left him and entered into Nathan Jesus who until then had only the provisional Ego rising from the unspoiled etheric body held back from Adam. Deprived of its human element, the Solomon child withered and died soon after. Nathan Jesus now consisted of the physical body descended from David through Joseph, the unspoiled etheric body held back from Adam, the purified astral body of the Buddha, and the most advanced Ego humanity had produced, that of the ancient Zarathustra and all it had accumulated through many succeeding incarnations—including the one as Zarathos who taught the middle period prophets in Babylon. One of these prophets, called "second Isaiah," had been able to foresee the birth of this great soul as the suffering servant that the Christ Spirit would use.

Composed as it was of these four elements, this advanced Ego and these three bodies, Nathan Jesus was able to utterly confound the teachers in the temple. But what is even more telling is that this so astonished his own parents. They were astonished because the simple child they had known up until that time was no longer merely pure, simple and deeply in touch with all creatures, but he was now wiser than the wisest in the temple as a mere twelve year old. Had this wisdom previously existed in the child, they would have come to expect this type of thing. As it is they too are incredulous.

When this remarkable fact is revealed to us, we then begin to see the deep wisdom that led the Evangelists to include only it in the thirty years between birth and ministry. But we have yet to exhaust the marvel.

We are told by Luke in a single verse that Jesus then increased in wisdom, age, and beauty—Luke's way of saying that the wise Ego worked on in these three bodies preparing them further for the next majestic event in the process of Incarnation, the entry of the Christ Spirit. The bodies would have to be magnificently prepared by this wise soul to withstand the entry of the intense, searing power of the Sun Spirit, the Son of God, the Christ.

But there were other developments in the families of the two boys. The Solomon Mary had other children, four sons and two daughters according to Mark's Gospel. The Solomon Joseph died, probably after fathering all of these children. Soon after the temple incident, the Nathan Mary also died. The two families merged by the marriage of the Solomon Mary to the Nathan Joseph, and all the children then lived together. In terms of Jesus' Ego, all his brothers and sisters were his own, as was his mother, while in terms of his body, he was the son of Joseph and lived in his native town of Nazareth.

This is the reason Luke says at the beginning of his genealogy that Jesus was the son, as was "supposed," of Joseph, for the Ego had originally incarnated in the Solomon Jesus and was not therefore connected fundamentally with the Nathan Joseph. We may also ponder the profound depth of Jesus' question, "Who is my mother, and who are my brothers?" It was especially profound since it was spoken after the further immense change brought about by his Baptism when, in respect of his all important Ego, as we shall see, he was no more related to any one person than to all others.

We are not done with family matters, for too much remains to be said about the Marys. Let us defer that momentarily, however, in order to look at the significance that numbers play in these two Nativity accounts.

We've already seen how Matthew starts with Abraham and counts forty-two generations in the development of the three bodies, a sevenfold process in each step. It seems strange that, in comparison, Luke goes all the way back to Adam in his genealogy, and in doing so lists a total of seventy-seven generations. If we examine this, we find that we move from the sevens of Matthew's Gospel to the twelves of Luke's; from the realm of the sevenfold planetary nature of our solar system into the twelvefold nature of the zodiac, a pattern one clearly sees in John's portrayal of the reascent of the human being in his Apocalypse. Time, or evolutionary development, is expressed in terms of seven, and timelessness in terms of twelve.

Above, forty-two generations were said to be necessary for the perfection of the three bodies of a descendent of Abraham that would be adequate to receive the Zarathustra Individuality. The requisite degree of perfection of the physical caused there to be a certain degree of perfection in the younger etheric and astral bodies, and thus could be considered the degree of perfection of the three. Steiner tells us that the Essenes recognized that a divine being, the Folk-Spirit of the Hebrew people, laid into the organic constitution of Abraham the seed for the bodies that were to descend from him, and that the seed was to work through the force of the blood, that is through heredity. Further, the Essenes perceived a spiritual law that the influence of heredity ceases only after forty-two stages: In other words, all traces of heredity have been eliminated from a human being's soul, and no influence exists, after forty-two generations. This was perceived as six cycles of seven generations, with the seventh cycle of seven representing the stage of perfection.

The hereditary aspects of the human body thus prepared for Zarathustra's return were mainly those of the physical body and the etheric body. The other two elements of the human being, the astral body and the Ego, would also have to be adequately prepared. For an event of such stupendous importance as the Incarnation this could not be accomplished by one personality, and two were necessary. This is entirely in line with the Essenic expectation of two Messiahs, one kingly

(Matthew) and one priestly (Luke). The physical body and the etheric body were prepared in the personality with whom Matthew's Gospel is primarily concerned; the astral body and Ego-principle were prepared in the personality of whom Luke's Gospel tells. Unfortunately, Steiner leaves us at this seemingly mystifying point. How is it that the physical and etheric bodies are said to relate to the Matthew account and the astral body and Ego to the Luke account when we have seen that the Zarathustra Ego of the Matthew account leaves the three bodies of the Solomon Jesus to enter the three bodies of the Nathan Jesus child of the Luke account? This is an example of where one must apply what is elsewhere given in order to make sense of the statement. We have already seen that the Solomon child was probably at least fourteen when the Nathan child was twelve. At fourteen, the Zarathustra Ego had utilized everything it acquired by inheritance by way of the physical and etheric bodies (seven years for each), and it was ready to enter into the period of development of the astral body (which commences at puberty). For that, it needed what was in the Nathan Jesus child. All development by the Zarathustra being from that point to the Baptism was in the three bodies of the Nathan Jesus.

Inasmuch as the physical and etheric bodies are related to the sevenfold solar system and time, the secret of six times seven applies to them, while the astral body and Ego relate to timelessness and to the zodiacal forces, so that the secret of eleven times seven applies to them. In each case, the final seven represents perfection. So in Matthew, the body prepared for the Solomon Jesus child (Zarathustra) is six times seven, or forty-two generations, while in Luke, the body prepared for the Nathan Jesus child (the unspoiled "Second Adam") is eleven times seven, or seventy-seven generations.

As explained in my longer work, generations prior to Abraham included many of what we would call generations, each one extending as long as the blood-enabled memory of a named ancestor's experiences continued.

We marvel that Luke dares to trace the genealogy of Jesus all the way back to God. But since Luke understood Adam to be the "first man," he would have started counting with him and not with God. That being so, it was necessary to insert one additional name, even though perhaps not historical (Arni and Admin being one, as noted earlier), in order to get to his vital number seventy-seven. In this manner we see clearly that Luke was not in error in presenting what he intended to say—which was *not earthly history* but *spiritual truth*.

That such was his intent seems clearly to be confirmed by the stress upon years in the prophetess Anna passage. We see there that Anna had lived a total of seventy-seven years either as a virgin or a widow (both of which have deep esoteric meaning relating to purity and devotion) and a total of eighty-four years ("great age," esoteric for wisdom) when she recognized the master. The name "Anna" comes from the Greek which in turn derives from the Hebrew *chana*, meaning "grace," and is expressed there in the name "Hannah" (and seems also related to the Jewish festival "Hanuka," which is literally *chanuka*). The number seventy-seven thus expresses humankind's perfecting process up to the final seven years, the twelfth septenary, which comes about by virtue of "grace." Here Luke merges the concepts seven and twelve in the number eighty-four, the product of the two.

Perhaps now we can begin to see the reason why Matthew left out three kings in his genealogy and why Luke made Ram into Arni and Admin in his. They were telling of spiritual development, to which earthly history was only subservient.

Before moving to the next event, it is noteworthy that not only did Essene prophecy, as discovered this century, predict two messiahs, but considerable early art work during the Christian era shows both Jesus children, as indicated in *The Burning Bush*.

From Jesus of Nazareth to Jesus Christ

It is the child that emerged in Luke's Gospel at twelve years of age when the two became one that is now properly called "Jesus of Nazareth" until the time of his Baptism at thirty years of age. For then an event awesome beyond words took place. At this moment, as John submersed Jesus of Nazareth in the River Jordan, the Zarathustra Individuality sacrificed itself, departing to make way for the Christ Spirit to enter, as Isaiah had foretold, into a servant human being. Every Gospel portrays this as a dove descending from heaven upon Jesus, and the synoptic Gospels all say that on this day Jesus was declared from the heavens to be the Son of God. This is when the Incarnation was consummated, though it remained until the Crucifixion for that Spirit to penetrate all the way into the very bones of Jesus, having only "lit upon him" to begin with. It was then said that these bones were not to be broken.

So it is at his Baptism that the one who became Jesus of Nazareth at twelve years of age becomes, in the above manner, Jesus Christ.

We may now understand why it is that Luke places his genealogy *after* the Baptism, immediately after, while Matthew places it before the earthly birth. For not until the Christ Spirit actually entered at Baptism was the Incarnation consummated, the Son of God was born on Earth, and that birth could only be understood by a genealogy that went all the way back to the event of Adam's birth.

With that thought, let us contemplate a point seldom noticed. To establish Bethlehem as the birthplace of the messiah, Matthew quotes from the fifth chapter of Micah:

And you, O Bethlehem, in the land of Judah, are by no means least among the rulers of Judah; for from you shall come a ruler who will govern my people Israel.

But he leaves off the last part of the prophecy which reads, "whose origin is from of old, from ancient days." We have seen how the ancient soul of Zarathustra was in Matthew's mind. While the Nathan Jesus child of Luke's Gospel was, as we have seen, in certain respects even more ancient, it was the soul of Zarathustra that lived in Jesus of Nazareth and sacrificed itself for the Christ. Moreover, the Nathan child had only a provisional Ego, and while old in a spiritual sense, in earthly terms it was very young. And the Christ did not enter in Bethlehem but at the River Jordan. So both the prophet and the Evangelist must have had a human soul in mind, the ancient servant-being, Zarathustra.

The Mystery of the Marys

Probably no part of the Nativity accounts has so offended the modern thinking person as that of the Virgin Birth, the Immaculate Conception and the Perpetual Virginity of Mary. However, anthroposophy shows us that it was literally a virgin birth and an immaculate conception, not because there was no physical union between the Josephs and the Marys but because of how the union came about and how the being of the primeval unspoiled soul of the Nathan Mary remained unspoiled throughout, her etheric body governing the nature of her physical body so as to either retain or restore her virginity. It was further "immaculate" in that she was not, because of her state of consciousness, subject to the same experience from union as in the case of other "fallen" human beings. The Solomon Mary is shown to have become a virgin when the Christ entered Jesus of Nazareth at the Baptism, for then the soul of Nathan Mary indwelt that of the Solomon Mary, transforming her bodies. While Steiner apparently never said so, there is also a mysterious implication in Matthew's passage saying that Joseph "knew her not until she had borne a son." Such "knowing" bears a firm resemblance to the infection of the astral body in the Garden where it says, "they *knew* that they were naked." In this sense, even the Solomon Mary may have remained virginal until after Jesus' birth when she conceived other children. This Mary, however, did not carry the primeval soul of the Nathan Mary at that time, so it seems possible that Matthew was telescoping into his abbreviated metaphor the result of what happened at the Baptism. In any event, anthroposophy now makes it possible to comprehend the Perpetual Virginity of Mary.

But there is another appealing possibility that would explain both the virginity of the Solomon Mary as well as Joseph's perplexity with her condition as Matthew sets them out. My friend Robert Powell writes of this, as cited in my larger work. He takes into account the visions of the illiterate nun Anne Catherine Emmerich (1774-1824). He shows their remarkable accuracy on items that are verifiable but far beyond the knowledge of all but the most scholarly students of the Jewish calender. At the same time he recognizes the inferiority of her visions to Steiner's intuition, including her failure to observe that two Jesus children were born. Because of this failure, she dismissed one of her visions indicating that the annunciation to the Solomon Mary took place in the temple, and not knowing of the *two* Marys she rejected this vision because of the annunciation to the Nathan Mary in Nazareth that took place later.

Emmerich's visions had included the fact that Mary had from a very young age been a "temple virgin," and still was at the time of the Conception while still a "young woman." According to Emmerich both the finding of a worthy prospective husband for, and then his betrothal to, this special temple virgin had been under the auspices of the temple's high priesthood. The very name "Joseph" suggests the clairvoyance of initiation, as with the patriarchal Joseph who was initiated into the Egyptian Mysteries. Here Powell infers from Emmerich's account the unique temple relationship of both Joseph and Mary, the appearance of the angel, and Joseph's later puzzlement, that in fact the betrothed couple had gone through the "temple sleep" (a death-like condition explained much more fully in *The Burning Bush*) under the guidance of its priesthood and conception had occurred during that time. There is something powerfully compelling about this in light of Matthew's account, "When Joseph woke from sleep, he did as the angel of the Lord commanded him; he took his wife, but knew her not until she had borne a son." It is said that Joseph had been told by an angel in a "dream" of Jesus' divine conception, but the dream could have been a part of the initiation process. Steiner shows us that dreams in that day belonged (or could still then belong) to the waking (fully conscious during "sleep") state while today they belong in the unreliable realm of sleep. Sensations pertaining to the body, such as are involved in the act of impregnation, would presumably not, however, intrude upon consciousness during the death-like "temple sleep," save perhaps in terms of spiritual ecstasy, as in The Song of Solomon.

THE INCREDIBLE BIRTHS OF JESUS

Emil Bock (1895-1959) as a young clergyman studied under Steiner and later wrote an eight volume presentation of Steiner's insights on the Bible. His *The Childhood of Jesus* covers the nativity accounts, as does the essay "The Nativity" in my larger work, *The Burning Bush*. The latter is intense, this shorter one more flowing, while Bock's is flowery in elegant expression of fine details buried within the two accounts I've set forth. His work would not by itself be readily accepted within Christendom, I think. It assumes a readership already exposed to anthroposophical insight, on the one hand, or willing to accept what could otherwise be called dreamy speculation, on the other.

This present volume represents something of a middle ground, with my detailed work on the right and Bock's more flowery one on the left. But his expressions do flesh out and bring to life the bony structure, once it has been built. He has the ability to put one back at the scene to observe how it all happened.

Conclusion

Rudolf Steiner stands at a fork in the road for humanity. Either what is made manifest by him about the Nativity and all that came therefrom is prophecy of the highest and most divine nature, or his teachings comprised some combination of abysmal ignorance and fraud.

From the earliest days of Christendom, the genealogies have been looked upon as inconsistent. Various attempts have been made to explain or reconcile, but all of these have been thoroughly discredited by eminent theological authorities. Only Steiner's account stands thoroughly plausible and consistent with everything that is set out in both Gospel accounts.

For the first time, the Biblical Nativity accounts are now revealed as a magnificent, consistent whole. One who contemplates the full implications of the Nativity as here presented must see in it anew the unspeakable majesty of Jesus Christ and therein the profoundly stimulating meaning and hope which is spoken by Isaiah:

> The people who walked in darkness have seen a great light; those who dwelt in a land of deep darkness, on them has light shined.
> Thou has multiplied the nation, thou hast increased its joy; they rejoice before thee as with joy at the harvest, as men rejoice when they divide the spoil.
> For the yoke of his burden, and the staff for his shoulder, the rod of his oppressor, thou hast broken as on the day of Midian.
> For every boot of the tramping warrior in battle tumult and every garment rolled in blood will be burned as fuel for the fire.
> For to us a child is born, to us a son is given; and the government will be upon his shoulder, and his name will be called "Wonderful Counselor, Mighty God, Everlasting Father, Prince of Peace."
> Of the increase of his government and of peace there will be no end, upon the throne of David, and over his kingdom, to establish it, and to uphold it with justice and with righteousness from this time forth and for evermore. The zeal of the Lord of hosts will do this.

EPILOGUE

Why Now?

Some may be able to accept what is said in the text without further ado. But others who have reached the end of the text above may be dogged by the question of how our particular time in history can be so crucial in the sense that only now is Christendom able to "bear" the truth in regard to the birth of Jesus (as well as countless other truths of Biblical revelation). The seeming similarity of the developmental pattern of Christianity and the individual human being, where centuries are to the former as years are to the latter, was pointed out in the text. But that is only a single circumstance, not alone sufficient for many minds.

For many, it will suffice simply to make a study of the history of Christendom prior to our time, for that alone should show the plausibility of the two millennial scenario here suggested. Europe's Middle Ages are called "dark" because they were, and little of spiritual light has come down to us from them. They do, in fact, span essentially the middle third of the time between Christ and the Twentieth Century. And while Aquinas searched existing written authority (and became thereby the theological anchor of Roman Catholicism to this day), and Christian mystics penetrated to divine personal experiences, nothing they handed down has brought enough new light to reverse the tendency to schism among sincerely devout persons and groups that marked the first six hundred years of Christian "brotherhood." Indeed, since the Renaissance, division within Christendom has proceeded apace with little indication of reversal save among confessions and denominations that have themselves suffered decline.

We speak today with great reverence for the Church Fathers. It is not entirely inappropriate that we do so, for they hammered out creeds and doctrines, and persevered to the point of even taking over civil government (the Roman, and Holy Roman, Empires) so as to first create and then preserve a tradition. But when the first six hundred years of the Christian era are examined, the overwhelming impression one gets, once the Apostolic Fathers of the first century were gone, is that it can best be described as a time of "isms" and schisms, devoid of real intuitive revelation, battles largely over the nature of the Christ (human, divine, or composite) and of the relationship between the Father, Son and Holy Spirit. In the final analysis, the conclusions are ecclesiastically legislated doctrine, hammered out under the protection, and in many cases under the mandate, of the Roman emperor with intrigue, bloodshed, intense hostility, and at best an uneasy peace to this day. It is hard not to see at work in this process the same attitude that existed between the Sadduccees, scribes and Pharisees in regard to the Mosaic law. In the name of Christ, and with the approbation of high authority, murder has been committed within the brotherhood not only in hammering out the early creeds and doctrines, but since then in persecution of so-called heretics, inquisition, and witchcraft (not limited to colonial America). The sword has been used in the name of Christ against pagans from the time of Constantine through the crusades of the Middle Ages and down to the wars in Lebanon, Bosnia and the like. The enormous good that has resulted from true Christian service down through the centuries cannot be denied. But that cannot itself justify a continued blindness to new revelation, for who can deny the need for a massive change in human thinking, feeling and willing in the direction of far greater collective good?

Christianity has always claimed to be "a revealed faith," and indeed it is. Christ and Paul both rejected the Judaistic idea that prophecy could be no more. Yet Christianity tends today to limit the "Word of God" to the canon and what can be gathered from a mere reading of that written word. But the nature of the revelation in that canon has yet to be understood—and for the sensitive soul the direction in which humanity is moving cries out for a revelation now of what Christ and "the Mystery of Golgotha" really meant for it. One who earnestly and sincerely studies the works of Rudolf Steiner can see this revelation and feel that the time of which Jeremiah spoke, when Christ would write his law upon human hearts (Jer 31,33-34), may be approaching.

All phenomena in our sensate world is prefigured by events in the spiritual world. This relates to John's description of the Logos, the Word, "all things were made through him, and without him was not anything made that was made" (Jn 1,3). It is the ability, through spiritual organs in some human beings developed far beyond those of their contemporaries, to perceive these events in the spiritual world. It is this that has always made prophecy possible. There were two of this type who stood above their contemporaries in this ability in the first century of our calendar, the Evangelist John and Paul. Almost all of the New Testament was written directly or indirectly by these two (when Luke and Acts are so considered, only two Gospels and the four non-Johannine letters fall outside this group).

Creative activity in the spiritual world is entirely under the domain of what doctrine calls "the Trinity," the Father, Son and Holy Spirit. However, between the Trinity and the four earthly kingdoms (human, animal, plant and mineral), and serving as agents of the Trinity, is what the Bible broadly calls the Heavenly Host. It too was "made" by the Logos. It comprises the nine ranks of the Hierarchies (from the Seraphim down to the angels) as well as discarnate spirits within the four earthly kingdoms. All of these intervening agencies include not only those who work for the purposes of the Trinity, but those fallen spirits who work for a time in opposition and whose actions are reflected on Earth in the form of evil.

An immense amount is encompassed in what has just been said, and is generally beyond the scope of this work (though considerably addressed in my longer work).

In *The Burning Bush* three major circumstances are given in some detail, each a distinct topic standing alone. The confluence of all three as our century opened is of great significance.

One such circumstance has to do with the end of the "dark ages," a far longer period of time than that associated with our own period of medieval history (the "Middle Ages"), one more nearly associated with the long period described by the Lord in answer to Isaiah's cry, "How long, O Lord" shall the eyes not see, the ears not hear and the heart not understand? (Is 6,11-13)—the human condition echoed in every Gospel, the conclusion of Acts, and the letter to the Romans. In the Orient, that dark age is said to be five thousand years long and to be called "Kali Yuga." The term is identical in meaning to the name "Deucalion" (hear the "calio" sound in each) found in the ancient Western myth Prometheus. The age started when the last vestige of true human communication with the spiritual world was being lost (when God was "hiding his face" to use Biblical terminology). The incredible memory of ancient times was fading, so that writing began to come into use—around 3,000 B.C. From then the five thousand years extended to the beginning of the third millennium, ending in 1899 according to Steiner. One does not have to look too hard to find evidence of the truth of this assertion and of the ancient myth.

A second circumstance has to do with the Second Coming of Christ, the *parousia* in Greek terminology. Luke tells us (Acts 1,11) that it shall be in the same body form as was the Ascension, the latter a topic largely ignored by Christian theology, though acknowledged by it and vital to it. It is even less understood than the mysterious nature of the appearances of the Risen Christ to some of his followers. Without an understanding of the three bodies of the human being, it is not possible to come to any real comprehension of either of these phenomena. According to Steiner the Second Coming of Christ is in the etheric world, having commenced there early in the twentieth century where it is already experienced by those whose organs are properly prepared, and the period will extend now for a long time while others, as suggested in John's Apocalypse ("they were each given a white robe and told to rest a little longer, until the number of their fellow servants and their brethren should be complete," Rev 6,11), develop this capacity by overcoming the veil of the flesh, the mineral-physical body. This topic (the Second Coming) is widely covered in the longer work, including by an entire essay. Only this brief summary can be given here.

It is the last of these three major spiritual events, all coinciding with the beginning of the twentieth century, that is of particular interest to us here. That event is the commencement of the new age (also called the "regency") of the

Archangel Michael, which Steiner placed late in the nineteenth century.

According to him, a divine law provides that the truths of real prophecy could never be truly recognized for a period of one hundred years after the life of the prophet. There is a reason for this, related to human egoism. In his provincial age, the Christ could express it more restrictively, "A prophet is not without honor except in his own country and in his own house" (Mt 13,57, Jn 4,44); today we must add, "or in his own time," given our shrinking world. When this law is applied, given Steiner's extensive revelations as our century opened, our present time takes on a significance far beyond that even normally associated with the end of a millennium.

Let us then turn our attention to Michael.

The Archangel Michael

The net result of the theology developed over the last two centuries is to consign to the genealogies of Jesus no significant meaning whatsoever, being at best an acknowledgment by the Evangelists of the expectation that Jesus was to be descended from David and an effort to show, however mysteriously, erroneously and inconsistently, how it was so. In truth Christendom came to this point almost from the beginning, though in the early centuries there was an instinctive recognition of their validity that was gradually lost with the passage of time up through the Renaissance. It had to be this way because they were among those things that humanity was not yet ready to understand, or could not "bear," to use Jesus' words. Only a divine Providence caused them to be perceived by the Evangelists who put them down for the day when a new light would begin to dawn, when, as

Jesus said, the Spirit of Truth would begin to work in humanity (Jn 16,12-13).

Up until the Renaissance there was within Christendom a high respect for the spiritual Hierarchies between the Trinity and humanity, from the Seraphim to the angels. As my larger work shows and as indicated in the text above, Paul was intimately acquainted with these and spoke of many of them in his letters. Dante and Aquinas, as well as numerous other Christian authorities, spoke of them. But with the evolution of human thinking since the Renaissance, knowledge of and faith in these spiritual ranks has been lost. It is most significant that only in the last few years has there been a reawakening within the human soul to the world of the angels. This phenomenon alone is a very real circumstance pointing to the irresistible, burgeoning power of the Spirit of Truth in our time.

While Steiner did not, to my knowledge, explicitly identify the Archangel Michael as the "Spirit of truth" referred to by Christ in Jn 16,13, presumably because at that stage his hearers were not yet ready for it, he nevertheless spoke so pointedly and so often of Michael in such terms as to lead us powerfully in that direction. And while he identified the year 1879 as the precise time that a "new age of Michael," his new "regency," the first since the days of Christ, commenced, he pointed to the end of the twentieth century and the beginning of the third millennium as a time of the greatest spiritual significance. So many things that he said have been corroborated by discoveries since his death that he seems to fulfill even the test prescribed for prophets during the period when prophecy was fading ("And if you say in your heart, 'How may we know the word which the Lord has spoken?'—when a prophet speaks in the name of the Lord, if the word does not come to pass or come true, that is a word which the Lord has not spoken," Deut 18,21-22).

In the main text above, it is shown that the first modern Bible commentary and the first modern introduction of the idea of reincarnation in the Western world were both focused upon the time surrounding the year 1879.

In its discussion of the term "paraclete," the Anchor Bible Dictionary (5 ABD 152) cites Christian scholars who either identify Michael with the Spirit of Truth (Betz) or as a model of the Johannine paraclete (Mowinckel, Johansson).

The Christian canon can hardly be interpreted other than as showing Michael to be the one spirit who alone stands with Christ for truth. Thus, Dan 10,21 says, "I will tell you what is inscribed in the book of truth: there is none who contends by my side against these ['the prince of the kingdom of Persia,' whom we may take to be the worldly powers] except Michael, your prince."

And in John's Apocalypse it is Michael who leads the fight against "the deceiver of the whole world" (Rev 12,7-9). Jude also recognizes "the archangel Michael" as the one "contending with the devil ... about the body of Moses." In the light of anthroposophical insight, one can more fully appreciate what is meant by "the body of Moses," seeing that it was a misunderstanding of the Mosaic law that led to the death of Christ ("If you believed Moses, you would believe me, for he wrote of me" Jn 5,46), and that it is the same literal, prosaic type of understanding of holy writ in our own day that so obscures the deeper, and seemingly mysterious, meanings of the Bible (cf. 2 Cor 3).

Moreover, it is widely recognized that Michael is the one Archangel Paul refers to ("For the Lord himself will descend from heaven with a cry of command, with the archangel's call, and with the sound of the trumpet of God," 1 Thess 4,16), as Steiner also has said, though the full meaning of this

Pauline verse awaits additional insight, as shown in *The Burning Bush.*

Christian scholars are virtually unanimous in recognizing the immense influence of the Book of Enoch upon the writers of the New Testament canon. At the time of Christ it had fallen into disuse among Hebrew authorities, but was looked upon as inspired scripture by many Christians. That it failed to enter the Christian canon can only be attributed to the fading of insight that would make it intelligible in the formalization process of the doctrines and canon of Christianity. One with anthroposophical insight will see in it a new blossoming of meaning in our time. It is virtually replete with references to Michael as the spokesman for truth among the heavenly powers.

Since few other than scholars have ready access to it, consider its following selected passages (taken from *The Ethiopic Book of Enoch,* London, Oxford University Press, 1978):

> **Enoch 20,1,5:**(1) And these are the names of the holy angels who keep watch.... (5) Michael, one of the holy angels, namely the one put in charge of the best part of mankind, in charge of the nation.

> **Enoch 24,3 through 25,3: 24** (3) And (there was) a seventh mountain in the middle of these, ... and fragrant trees surrounded it. (4) And there was among them a tree such as I have never smelt, and none of them nor any others were like it: it smells more fragrant than any fragrance, and its leaves and its flowers and its wood never wither; its fruit (is) good, and its fruit (is) like the bunches of dates on a palm. (5) And then I said: "Behold, this beautiful tree? Beautiful to look at and pleasant (are) its leaves, and its fruit very delightful in

appearance." (6) And then Michael, one of the holy and honored angels who was with me and (was) in charge of them, answered me 25 (1) and said to me: "Enoch why do you ask me about the fragrance of this tree, and (why) do you inquire to learn?" (2) Then I, Enoch, answered him, saying: "I wish to learn about everything, but especially about this tree." (3) And he answered me, saying: "This high mountain which you saw, whose summit is like the throne of the Lord, is the throne where the Holy and Great One, the Lord of Glory, the Eternal King, will sit when he comes to visit the earth for good."

Enoch 40,8-10:(8) And after this I asked the angel of peace who went with me and showed me everything which is secret: "Who are these four figures whom I have seen and whose words I have heard and written down?" (9) And he said to me: "This first one is the holy Michael, the merciful and long-suffering; and the second, who (is) in charge of all the diseases and in charge of all the wounds of the sons of men, is Raphael; and the third, who (is) in charge of all the powers, is the holy Gabriel; and the fourth, who (is) in charge of the repentance (leading) to hope of those who will inherit eternal life, is Phanuel." (10) And these (are) the four angels of the Lord Most High; and the four voices I heard in those days."

Enoch 69,14-15: (14) And this one told the holy Michael that he should show *him* the secret name, *that they might mention it in the oath*, so that those who showed the sons of men everything which is secret trembled before that name and oath. (15) And this (is) the power of this oath, for it is powerful and strong; and he placed this oath *Akae* [cf. "Akashic" in *The Burning Bush*] in the charge of the holy Michael. [My emphasis]

Enoch 71,3-4: (3) And the angel Michael, one of the archangels, took hold of me by my right hand, and raised me, and led me out to all the secrets of mercy and the secrets of righteousness. (4) And he showed me all the secrets of the ends of heaven and all the storehouses of all the stars and the lights, from where they come out before the holy ones.

(Michael is also referred to in chapters 60, 67, 68 and later in 71, but the above seem most relevant.)

In accordance with the sevenfold nature of creation (Prov 9,1), there are seven Archangels (Enoch 24 had spoken of "seven mountains" with Michael speaking, as above, in regard to the "seventh") among whom Michael is acknowledged as supreme, he who is associated with the Sun. There is a sevenfold series of regencies, one for each successive Archangel, each one being something over three hundred years. Whether they are precisely equal or only approximately so has not been made clear, even by Steiner. In the fifteenth century, Johannes Tritheim, the abbot of Sponheim, is said to have determined each archangelic period to be 354 1/3 years long. Perhaps significantly this is precisely one hundred times the length of twelve lunar synodic months (354 1/3 days each). If he is right and the current age of Michael began in 1879, then the prior age would have run from 601 to 247 B.C., encompassing, as Steiner indicated, the Greek sages Heraclitus, Socrates, Plato and Aristotle as well as the spreading of Greek civilization by Alexander in divine preparation for Paul's evangelization of the Greek world. We know of Plato's influence upon John's Gospel. Socrates and Heraclitus were both singled out by Justin Martyr (ca. A.D. 100-165) as Christians before the incarnation of Christ.

Not only did the critical study of modern theology begin around 1879, but the twentieth century has witnessed an explosion in human discovery of all kinds, including the Dead Sea Scrolls, the Nag Hammadi library, and numerous other artifacts providentially buried until the time was right for their revelation. Conceivably the most significant of these is the mid-century discovery of the so-called "Secret Gospel of Mark," discussed more fully in *The Burning Bush*, widely known among theologians but whose full meaning has yet to be apprehended by those not familiar with Steiner's own revelations.

With these things in mind, let us look at some of what Steiner says about Michael and his "new age."

That approximately three hundred fifty year "age" began, imperceptibly to most, to dawn in 1879. The last age of the Archangel Michael was before the time of Christ when the enlightenment of Plato and Aristotle was spread by Alexander over the area that the Apostle Paul was to evangelize in the Greek language. It is hard to imagine how Christianity could have been spread without that development.

Human understanding of the Christ, and of its own nature, had to wait then until the age of the highest Archangel returned again, the Archangel that Hebrew and Christian tradition has always associated with the Sun. It is Michael that strives with and for the Christ to administer the divine intelligence to humanity. And so when Christ spoke of the Spirit of Truth coming, it was of the time when the regency of the Archangel Michael would again return, as Daniel indicates.

It is symptomatic that the first stirrings in the development of modern theology and the first overt introduction of the concept of reincarnation in the West in modern times took place then. Steiner was eighteen years old in 1879, and at the turn of the century began to plant in human evolution his vast spiritual intuitions. Michael was beginning to rouse humanity from its slumber. But even then Steiner said that a momentous and critical time would follow upon the turn of the millennium ending the twentieth century. We are there.

In the fall of last year, 1997, my book *The Burning Bush*, was published by the Anthroposophic Press, Hudson, NY. As the first Bible commentary[2] written to show the Bible's deeper meaning in the light of Steiner's teachings, called "anthroposophy," it attempts to bring into mainline Christendom magnificent new insights. Never before mentioned or cited to my knowledge in any Bible commentary, the gift of this true prophet needs now, three quarters of a century after his death, to come into the mind of those who are destined to lead Christianity forward on its upward path. When it does, Christianity can become more than one of the Earth's divisive religions. The Sun of Christianity can begin truly to shine upon all creation.

The day will come, and is hopefully not too far distant, when Christendom will look back upon its Biblical understandings of the nineteenth and twentieth centuries much as we today look back upon that of prior centuries, even of the dark ages. We will come back to a respect for what Plato gave to humanity in the prior age of Michael. The insights of that

---

2. Some early European writings might be loosely called "commentaries" on the Bible, or portions of it, but in general they were calculated to have meaning only to those already having some familiarity with Steiner's work, and most of them were by persons who were clergy before they met Steiner and who could relate his teachings to the Bible for the benefit of others less biblically oriented. Examples include works by Emil Bock, Rudolf Frieling, Friedrich Rittelmeyer, all of whom were clergy, and the controversial Valentin Tomberg.

age were reflected in the works of the leading Jewish and early Christian theologians in Alexandria. Many of these works, such as those of Origen who recognized the pre-existence of the soul, were destroyed by the early Church. Their insight must be regained and transformed to an even greater lustre than before, irradiated by the divine intelligence administered by Michael as an agent of Christ. For during the prior regency of Michael, the divine intelligence could not be brought to Earth inasmuch as the Christ had yet to walk the Earth in the flesh and spill into it his blood.

With that said, let us return to the matter of the descent of Jesus from David. Much has been discovered during this century, providentially hidden until now, that corroborates things Steiner said long before the discoveries. One of them is the Essenic expectation of two Messiahs, one kingly and one priestly. That expectation, vindicated by historical fact, was then reflected in the two Gospel accounts. The reason they seem to be in conflict is that they have thus far been assumed to tell of the birth of a single Jesus child. But their many differences reveal to us now that they tell quite accurately of the birth of two Jesus children, quite different in nature, each born to parents named Mary and Joseph. In both Gospels the angel gives the child's name as Jesus. Whether both sets of parents originally bore the names Mary and Joseph, or whether they were given those names as a result of the function they performed, as happened with almost every major Biblical character, is not really important. In truth, they were both Mary and Joseph just as Jacob was Israel, Simon was Peter and Saul was Paul.

Biblical Accounts of the Births of Jesus

ACCORDING TO THE TRADITIONAL
KING JAMES VERSION

(American spelling, and omitting accent markings)

THE GOSPEL ACCORDING TO MATTHEW

Chapters One and Two

1

(1) THE book of the generation of Jesus Christ, the son of David, the son of Abraham.

(2) Abraham begat Isaac; and Isaac begat Jacob; and Jacob begat Judas and his brethren;

(3) And Judas begat Phares and Zara of Tha-mar; and Phares begat Esrom; and Esrom began A-ram;

(4) And A-ram begat A-min-a-dab; and A-min-a-dab begat Na-as-son; and Na-as-son begat Sal-mon;

(5) And Sal-mon begat Bo-oz of Ra-chab; and Bo-oz begat O-bed of Ruth; and O-bed begat Jesse;

(6) And Jesse begat David the king; and David the king begat Solomon of her that had been the wife of U-ri-as;

(7) And Solomon begat Ro-bo-am; and Ro-bo-am begat A-bi-a; and A-bi-a begat A-sa;

(8) And A-sa begat Jos-a-phat; and Jos-a-phat begat Jo-ram; and Jo-ram begat O-zi-as;

(9) And O-zi-as begat Jo-a-tham; and Jo-a-tham begat A-chaz; and A-chaz begat Ez-e-ki-as;

(10) And Ez-e-ki-as begat Ma-nas-ses; and Ma-nas-ses begat Amon; and Amon begat Jo-si-as;

(11) And Jo-si-as begat Jech-o-ni-as and his brethren, about the time they were carried away to Babylon:

(12) And after they were brought to Babylon, Jech-o-ni-as begat Sa-la-thi-el; and Sa-la-thi-el begat Zo-rob-a-bel;

(13) And Zo-rob-a-bel begat A-bi-ud; and A-bi-ud begat E-li-a-kim; and E-li-a-kim begat A-zor;

(14) And A-zor begat Sa-doc; and Sa-doc begat A-chim; and A-chim begat E-li-ud;

(15) And E-li-ud begat E-le-a-zar; and E-le-a-zar begat Mat-than; and Mat-than begat Jacob;

(16) And Jacob begat Joseph the husband of Mary, of whom was born Jesus, who is called Christ.

(17) So all the generations from Abraham to David are fourteen generations; and from David until the carrying away into Babylon are fourteen generations; and from the carrying away into Babylon unto Christ are fourteen generations.

(18) Now the birth of Jesus Christ was on this wise: When as his mother Mary was espoused to Joseph, before they came together, she was found with child of the Holy Ghost.

(19) Then Joseph her husband, being a just man, and not willing to make her a public example, was minded to put her away privily.

(20) But while he thought on these things, behold, the angel of the Lord appeared unto him in a dream, saying, Joseph, thou son of David, fear not to take unto thee Mary thy wife: for that which is conceived in her is of the Holy Ghost.

(21) And she shall bring forth a son, and thou shalt call his name Jesus: for he shall save his people from their sins.

(22) Now all this was done, that it might be fulfilled which was spoken of the Lord by the prophet, saying,

(23) BEHOLD, a virgin shall be with child, and shall bring forth a son, and they shall call his name EM-MAN-U-EL, which being interpreted is, God with us.

(24) Then Joseph being raised from sleep did as the angel of the Lord had bidden him, and took unto him his wife:

(25) And knew her not till she had brought forth her first-born son: and he called his name Jesus.

2

(1) NOW when Jesus was born in Beth-le-hem of Ju-dae-a in the days of Herod the king, behold, there came wise men from the east to Jerusalem,

(2) Saying, Where is he that is born King of the Jews? for we have seen his star in the east, and are come to worship him.

(3) When Herod the king had heard these things, he was troubled, and all Jerusalem with him.

(4) And when he had gathered all the chief priests and scribes of the people together, he demanded of them where Christ should be born.

(5) And they said unto him, In Beth-le-hem of Ju-dae-a: for thus it is written by the prophet,

(6) AND thou Beth-le-hem, in the land of Juda, art not the least among the princes of Juda: for out of thee shall come a governor, that shall rule my people Israel.

(7) Then Herod, when he had privily called the wise men, enquired of them diligently what time the star appeared.

(8) And he sent them to Beth-le-hem, and said, Go and search diligently for the young child; and when ye have found him, bring me word again, that I may come and worship him also.

(9) When they had heard the king, they departed; and, lo, the star, which they saw in the east, went before them, till it came and stood over where the young child was.

(10) When they saw the star, they rejoiced with exceeding great joy.

(11) And when they were come into the house, they saw the young child with Mary his mother, and fell down, and worshipped him: and when they had opened their treasures, they presented unto him gifts; gold, and frankincense, and myrrh.

(12) And being warned of God in a dream that they should not return to Herod, they departed into their own country another way.

(13) And when they were departed, behold, the angel of the Lord appeareth to Joseph in a dream, saying, Arise, and take the young child and his mother, and flee into Egypt, and be thou there until I bring thee word: for Herod will seek the young child to destroy him.

(14) When he arose, he took the young child and his mother by night, and departed into Egypt:

(15) And was there until the death of Herod: that it might be fulfilled which was spoken of the Lord by the prophet, saying, Out of Egypt have I called my son.

(16) Then Herod, when he saw that he was mocked of the wise men, was exceeding wroth, and sent forth, and slew all the children that were in Beth-le-hem, and in all the coasts thereof, from two years old and under, according to the time which he had diligently enquired of the wise men.

(17) Then was fulfilled that which was spoken by Jeremy, the prophet, saying,

(18) IN ra-ma was there a voice heard, lamentation, and weeping, and great mourning, Ra-chel weeping for her children, and would not be comforted, because they are not.

(19) But when Herod was dead, behold, an angel of the Lord appeareth in a dream to Joseph in Egypt,

(20) Saying, Arise, and take the young child and his mother, and go into the land of Israel: for they are dead which sought the young child's life.

(21) And he arose, and took the young child and his mother, and came into the land of Israel.

(22) But when he heard that Ar-che-la-us did reign in Ju-dae-a in the room of his father Herod, he was afraid to go thither: notwithstanding, being warned of God in a dream, he turned aside into the parts of Galilee:

(23) And he came and dwelt in a city called Nazareth: that it might be fulfilled which was spoken by the prophets, He shall be called a Nazarene.

THE GOSPEL ACCORDING TO LUKE

Chapters One and Two and Verses Twenty-Three Through Thirty-Eight of Chapter Three

1

(1) FORASMUCH as many have taken in hand to set forth in order a declaration of those things which are most surely believed among us,

(2) Even as they delivered them unto us, which from the beginning were eyewitnesses, and ministers of the word;

(3) It seemed good to me also, having had perfect understanding of all things from the very first, to write unto thee in order, most excellent The-oph-i-lus,

(4) That thou mightest know the certainty of those things, wherein thou hast been instructed.

(5) There was in the days of Herod, the king of Ju-dae-a, a certain priest named Zach-a-ri-as, of the course of A-bi-a: and his wife was of the daughters of Aaron, and her name was Elizabeth.

(6) And they were both righteous before God, walking in all the commandments and ordinances of the Lord blameless.

(7) And they had no child, because that Elizabeth was barren, and they both were now well stricken in years.

(8) And it came to pass, that while he executed the priest's office before God in the order of his course,

(9) According to the custom of the priest's office, his lot was to burn incense when he went into the temple of the Lord.

(10) And the whole multitude of the people were praying without at the time of incense.

(11) And there appeared unto him an angel of the Lord standing on the right side of the altar of incense.

(12) And when Zach-a-ri-as saw him, he was troubled, and fear fell upon him.

(13) But the angel said unto him, Fear not, Zach-a-ri-as: for thy prayer is heard; and thy wife Elizabeth shall bear thee a son, and thou shalt call his name John.

(14) And thou shalt have joy and gladness; and many shall rejoice at his birth.

(15) For he shall be great in the sight of the Lord, and shall drink neither wine nor strong drink; and he shall be filled with the Holy Ghost, even from his mother's womb.

(16) And many of the children of Israel shall he turn to the Lord their God.

(17) AND he shall go before him in the spirit and power of E-li-as, to turn the hearts of the fathers to the children, and the disobedient to the wisdom of the just; to make ready a people prepared for the Lord.

(18) And Zach-a-ri-as said unto the angel, Whereby shall I know this? for I am an old man, and my wife well stricken in years.

(19) And the angel answering said unto him, I am Gabriel, that stand in the presence of God; and am sent to speak unto thee, and to shew thee these glad tidings.

(20) And, behold, thou shalt be dumb, and not able to speak, until the day that these things shall be performed, because thou believest not my words, which shall be fulfilled in their season.

(21) And the people waited for Zach-a-ri-as, and marvelled that he tarried so long in the temple.

(22) And when he came out, he could not speak unto them: and they perceived that he had seen a vision in the temple: for he beckoned unto them, and remained speechless.

(23) And it came to pass, that, as soon as the days of his ministration were accomplished, he departed to his own house.

(24) And after those days his wife Elizabeth conceived, and hid herself five months, saying,

(25) Thus hath the Lord dealt with me in the days wherein he looked on me, to take away my reproach among men.

(26) And in the sixth month the angel Gabriel was sent from God unto a city of Galilee, named Nazareth,

(27) To a virgin espoused to a man whose name was Joseph, of the house of David; and the virgin's name was Mary.

(28) And the angel came in unto her, and said, Hail, thou that art highly favored, the Lord is with thee: blessed art thou among women.

(29) And when she saw him, she was troubled at his saying, and cast in her mind what manner of salutation this should be.

(30) And the angel said unto her, Fear not, Mary: for thou hast found favor with God.

(31) And, behold, thou shalt conceive in thy womb, and bring forth a son, and shalt call his name Jesus.

(32) He shall be great, and shall be called Son of the Highest: and the Lord God shall give unto him the throne of his father David:

(33) And he shall reign over the house of Jacob for ever; and of his kingdom there shall be no end.

(34) Then said Mary unto the angel, How shall this be, seeing I know not a man?

(35) And the angel answered and said unto her, The Holy Ghost shall come upon thee, and the power of the Highest shall overshadow thee: therefore also that holy thing which shall be born of thee shall be called the Son of God.

(36) And, behold, thy cousin Elizabeth, she hath also conceived a son in her old age: and this is the sixth month with her, who was called barren.

(37) For with God nothing shall be impossible.

(38) And Mary said, Behold the handmaid of the Lord; be it unto me according to thy word. And the angel departed from her.

(39) And Mary arose in those days, and went into the hill country with haste, into a city of Juda;

(40) And entered into the house of Zach-a-ri-as, and saluted Elizabeth.

(41) And it came to pass, that, when Elizabeth heard the salutation of Mary, the babe leaped in her womb; and Elizabeth was filled with the Holy Ghost:

(42) And she spake out with a loud voice, and said, Blessed art thou among women, and blessed is the fruit of thy womb.

(43) And whence is this to me, that the mother of my Lord should come to me?

(44) For, lo, as soon as the voice of thy salutation sounded in mine ears, the babe leaped in my womb for joy.

(45) And blessed is she that believed: for there shall be a performance of those things which were told her from the Lord.

(46) And Mary said, My soul doth magnify the Lord,

(47) And my spirit hath rejoiced in God my Savior.

(48) For he hath regarded the low estate of his handmaiden: for, behold, from henceforth all generations shall call me blessed.

(49) For he that is mighty hath done to me great things; and holy is his name.

(50) And his mercy is on them that fear him from generation to generation.

(51) He hath shewed strength with his arm; he hath scattered the proud in the imagination of their hearts.

(52) He hath put down the mighty from their seats, and exalted them of low degree.

(53) He hath filled the hungry with good things; and the rich he hath sent empty away.

(54) He hath helped his servant Israel, in remembrance of his mercy;

(55) As he spake to our fathers, to Abraham, and his seed for ever.

(56) And Mary abode with her about three months, and returned to her own house.

(57) Now Elizabeth's full time came that she should be delivered; and she brought forth a son.

(58) And her neighbors and her cousins heard how the Lord had showed great mercy upon her; and they rejoiced with her.

(59) And it came to pass, that on the eighth day they came to circumcise the child; and they called him Zach-a-ri-as, after the name of his father.

(60) And his mother answered and said, Not so; but he shall be called John.

(61) And they said unto her, There is none of thy kindred that is called by this name.

(62) And they made signs to his father, how he would have him called.

(63) And he asked for a writing table, and wrote, saying, His name is John. And they marvelled all.

(64) And his mouth was opened immediately, and his tongue loosed, and he spake, and praised God.

(65) And fear came on all that dwelt round about them: and all these sayings were noised abroad throughout all the hill country of Ju-dae-a.

(66) And all they that heard them laid them up in their hearts, saying, What manner of child shall this be! And the hand of the Lord was with him.

(67) And his father Zach-a-ri-as was filled with the Holy Ghost, and prophesied, saying,

(68) Blessed be the Lord God of Israel; for he hath visited and redeemed his people,

(69) And hath raised up an horn of salvation for us in the house of his servant David;

(70) As he spake by the mouth of his holy prophets, which have been since the world began:

(71) That we should be saved from our enemies, and from the hand of all that hate us;

(72) To perform the mercy promised to our fathers, and to remember his holy covenant;

(73) The oath which he swore to our father Abraham,

(74) That he would grant unto us, that we, being delivered out of the hand of our enemies, might serve him without fear,

(75) In holiness and righteousness before him, all the days of our life.

(76) And thou, child, shalt be called the prophet of the Highest: for thou shalt go before the face of the Lord to prepare his ways;

(77) To give knowledge of salvation unto his people by the remission of their sins,

(78) Through the tender mercy of our God; whereby the dayspring from on high hath visited us,

(79) To give light to them that sit in darkness and in the shadow of death, to guide our feet into the way of peace.

(80) And the child grew, and waxed strong in spirit, and was in the deserts till the day of his showing unto Israel.

2

(1) AND it came to pass in those days, that there went out a decree from Caesar Augustus, that all the world should be taxed.

(2) (And this taxing was first made when Cy-re-ni-us was governor of Syria.)

(3) And all went to be taxed, every one into his own city.

(4) And Joseph also went up from Galilee, out of the city of Nazareth, into Ju-dae-a, unto the city of David, which is called Beth-le-hem; (because he was of the house and lineage of David:)

(5) To be taxed with Mary his espoused wife, being great with child.

(6) And so it was, that, while they were there, the days were accomplished that she should be delivered.

(7) And she brought forth her firstborn son, and wrapped him in swaddling clothes, and laid him in a manger; because there was no room for them in the inn.

(8) And there were in the same country shepherds abiding in the field, keeping watch over their flock by night.

(9) And, lo, the angel of the Lord came upon them, and the glory of the Lord shone round about them: and they were sore afraid.

(10) And the angel said unto them, Fear not: for, behold, I bring you good tidings of great joy, which shall be to all people.

(11) For unto you is born this day in the city of David a Savior, which is Christ the Lord.

(12) And this shall be a sign unto you; Ye shall find the babe wrapped in swaddling clothes, lying in a manger.

(13) And suddenly there was with the angel a multitude of the heavenly host praising God, and saying,

(14) Glory to God in the highest, and on earth peace, good will toward men.

(15) And it came to pass, as the angels were gone away from them into heaven, the shepherds said one to another, Let us now go even unto Beth-le-hem, and see this thing which is come to pass, which the Lord hath made known unto us.

(16) And they came with haste, and found Mary, and Joseph, and the babe lying in a manger.

(17) And when they had seen it, they made known abroad the saying which was told them concerning this child.

(18) And all they that heard it wondered at those things which were told them by the shepherds.

(19) But Mary kept all these things, and pondered them in her heart.

(20) And the shepherds returned, glorifying and praising God for all the things that they had heard and seen, as it was told unto them.

(21) And when eight days were accomplished for the circumcising of the child, his name was called Jesus, which was so named of the angel before he was conceived in the womb.

(22) And when the days of her purification according to the law of Moses were accomplished, they brought him to Jerusalem, to present him to the Lord;

(23) (As it is written in the law of the Lord, every male that openeth the womb shall be called holy to the lord;)

(24) And to offer a sacrifice according to that which is said in the law of the Lord, a pair of turtledoves, or two young pigeons.

(25) And, behold, there was a man in Jerusalem, whose name was Simeon; and the same man was just and devout, waiting for the consolation of Israel: and the Holy Ghost was upon him.

(26) And it was revealed unto him by the Holy Ghost, that he should not see death, before he had seen the Lord's Christ.

(27) And he came by the Spirit into the temple: and when the parents brought in the child Jesus, to do for him after the custom of the law,

(28) Then took he him up in his arms, and blessed God, and said,

(29) Lord, now lettest thou thy servant depart in peace, according to thy word:

(30) For mine eyes have seen thy salvation,

(31) Which thou hast prepared before the face of all people;

(32) A light to lighten the Gentiles, and the glory of thy people Israel.

(33) And Joseph and his mother marvelled at those things which were spoken of him.

(34) And Simeon blessed them, and said unto Mary his mother, Behold this child is set for the fall and rising again of many in Israel; and for a sign which shall be spoken against;

(35) (Yea, a sword shall pierce through thy own soul also,) that the thoughts of many hearts may be revealed.

(36) And there was one Anna, a prophetess, the daughter of Phan-u-el, of the tribe of A-ser: she was of a great age, and had lived with an husband seven years from her virginity;

(37) And she was a widow of about fourscore and four years, which departed not from the temple, but served God with fastings and prayers night and day.

(38) And she coming in that instant gave thanks likewise unto the Lord, and spake of him to all them that looked for redemption in Jerusalem.

(39) And when they had performed all things according to the law of the Lord, they returned into Galilee, to their own city Nazareth.

(40) And the child grew, and waxed strong in spirit, filled with wisdom: and the grace of God was upon him.

(41) Now his parents went to Jerusalem every year at the feast of the passover.

(42) And when he was twelve years old, they went up to Jerusalem after the custom of the feast.

(43) And when they had fulfilled the days, as they returned, the child Jesus tarried behind in Jerusalem; and Joseph and his mother knew not of it.

(44) But they, supposing him to have been in the company, went a day's journey; and they sought him among their kinsfolk and acquaintance.

(45) And when they found him not, they turned back again to Jerusalem, seeking him.

(46) And it came to pass, that after three days they found him in the temple, sitting in the midst of the doctors, both hearing them, and asking them questions.

(47) And all that heard him were astonished at his understanding and answers.

(48) And when they saw him, they were amazed: and his mother said unto him, Son, why hast thou thus dealt with us? behold, thy father and I have sought thee sorrowing.

(49) And he said unto them, How is it that ye sought me? wist ye not that I must be about my Father's business?

(50) And they understood not the saying which he spake unto them.

(51) And he went down with them, and came to Nazareth, and was subject unto them: but his mother kept all these sayings in her heart.

(52) And Jesus increased in wisdom and stature, and in favor with God and man.

3 . . .

(23) And Jesus himself began to be about thirty years of age, being (as was supposed) the son of Joseph, which was the son of He-li,

(24) Which was the son of Mat-that, which was the son of Levi, which was the son of Mel-chi, which was the son of Janna, which was the son of Joseph,

(25) Which was the son of Mat-ta-thi-as, which was the son of Amos, which was the son of Na-um, which was the son of Es-li, which was the son of Nag-ge,

(26) Which was the son of Ma-ath, which was the son of Ma-ta-thi-as, which was the son of Sem-e-i, which was the son of Joseph, which was the son of Juda.

(27) Which was the son of Jo-an-na, which was the son of Rhe-sa, which was the son of Zo-rob-a-bel, which was the son of Sa-la-thi-el, which was the son of Ne-ri,

(28) Which was the son of Mel-chi, which was the son of Ad-di, which was the son of Co-sam, which was the son of El-mo-dam, which was the son of Er,

(29) Which was the son of Jo-se, which was the son of E-li-e-zer, which was the son of Jo-rim, which was the son of Mat-that, which was the son of Levi,

(30) Which was the son of Simeon, which was the son of Juda, which was the son of Joseph, which was the son of Jo-nan, which was the son of E-li-a-kim,

(31) Which was the son of Me-le-a, which was the son of Me-nan, which was the son of Mat-ta-tha, which was the son of Nathan, which was the son of David,

(32) Which was the son of Jesse, which was the son of O-bed, which was the son of Bo-oz, which was the son of Sal-mon, which was the son of Na-as-son,

(33) Which was the son of A-min-a-dab, which was the son of A-ram, which was the son of Es-rom, which was the son of Pha-res, which was the son of Juda,

(34) Which was the son of Jacob, which was the son of Isaac, which was the son of Abraham, which was the son of Tha-ra, which was the son of Na-chor,

(35) Which was the son of Sa-ruch, which was the son of Ra-gau, which was the son of Pha-lec, which was the son of He-ber, which was the son of Sa-la,

(36) Which was the son of Ca-i-nan, which was the son of Ar-phax-ad, which was the son of Sem, which was the son of No-e, which was the son of La-mech,

(37) Which was the son of Ma-thu-sa-la, which was the son of E-noch, which was the son of Ja-red, which was the son of Ma-le-le-el, which was the son of Ca-i-nan,

(38) Which was the son of E-nos, which was the son of Seth, which was the son of Adam, which was the son of God.

ABOUT THE AUTHOR

Edward Reaugh Smith, an Illinoian transplanted to Texas at mid-century, husband, father, and grandfather, has had broad interests in life. Successful lawyer and businessman, amateur musician and athlete, his lifelong search for the deeper meaning of the Bible, which he taught for over twenty-five years before discovering the writings of Rudolf Steiner, expresses itself in this work.

The Burning Bush

EDWARD REAUGH SMITH

More significant for Christianity in the twentieth-century than the discoveries of the Nag Hammadi and the Dead Sea Scrolls is the growing American awareness of the works of Rudolf Steiner. Practically unavailable until recently, English translations of his works from the German archives are now gradually coming into print.

Until *The Burning Bush* no Bible commentary had incorporated the remarkable spiritual insights of anthroposophy. Now, Edward Reaugh Smith combines his own extensive knowledge of traditional biblical scholarship with years of concentrated study of hundreds of Steiner titles. The result is, for the first time ever, a Bible commentary informed by anthroposophical insight.

Because of its radical newness, *The Burning Bush,* as an introductory volume to a complete series, deviates from the normal commentary mode, presenting a series of essays on terms and phrases of critical importance to a deeper comprehension of the biblical message. It includes an extensive bibliography of Steiner's works as well as numerous charts, diagrams, and cross-references, making this a tremendously valuable research tool.

In an extraordinary feat of scholarship, Edward R. Smith shows how the Anthroposophical writings and lectures of Rudolf Steiner clarify many of the major mysteries of the Bible. Steiner's mission, he declares, was to reintroduce into Western thinking and Christianity the tandem concepts of reincarnation and karma. He substantiates his assertions with his encyclopedic knowledge of both the Bible and the writings of Steiner, which he flawlessly integrates in The Burning Bush.

–Donald Melcer, Ph.D.,
Professor Emeritus, Michigan State University, Licensed Psychologist.

Anthroposophic Press
800 pages, paperback   hardback
ISBN 0-88010-447-3   ISBN 0-88010-449-X
Book #2085   Book # 2096
$29.95 $34.95